Important facts

This **Law Pack** Guide contains the information and instructions necessary to make or defend a personal injury claim. This Guide is for use in England or Wales. It is not suitable for use in Scotland or Northern Ireland.

The information it contains has been carefully compiled from professional sources, but its accuracy is not guaranteed, as laws and regulations may change or be subject to differing interpretations.

Neither this nor any other publication can take the place of a solicitor on important legal matters. As with any legal matter, common sense should determine whether you need the assistance of a solicitor rather than rely solely on the information and forms in this **Law Pack** Guide.

We strongly urge you to consult a solicitor if:

- substantial amounts of money are involved;
- you do not understand the instructions or are uncertain how to complete and use a form correctly;
- what you want to do is not precisely covered by this Guide.

Exclusion of Liability and Disclaimer

This book is sold with the understanding that neither the author nor the publisher is engaged in rendering legal advice. If legal advice is required, the services of a solicitor should be sought. The publisher and the author cannot in any way guarantee that the forms in this book are being used for the purposes intended and, therefore, assume no responsibility for their proper and correct use.

Whilst every effort has been made to ensure that this **Law Pack** Guide provides accurate and expert guidance, it is impossible to predict all the circumstances in which it may be used. Accordingly, neither the publisher, author, retailers nor any other suppliers shall be liable to any person or entity with respect to any loss or damage caused or alleged to be caused by the information contained in or omitted from this **Law Pack** Guide.

Do-it-yourself

PERSONAL INJURY CLAIMS

LAWPACK™
GUIDE

Personal Injury Claims
by Felicity Mileham

© 2001 Law Pack Publishing Limited

Law Pack Publishing Limited
76-89 Alscot Road
London SE1 3AW

www.lawpack.co.uk

Printed in Great Britain

ISBN: 1 902646 59 2

Table of contents

How to use this Law Pack Guide

This **Law Pack** Guide can help you achieve an important legal objective conveniently, efficiently and economically. Remember that it is important for you to use this guide properly if you are to avoid later difficulties.

Step-by-step instructions for using this guide:

1. Read this guide carefully. If after thorough examination you decide that your requirements are not met by this **Law Pack** Guide, or you do not feel confident about writing your own documents, consult a solicitor.

2. In this guide are example forms and documentation, for reference when preparing your own.

3. When completing a form, do not leave any section blank, unless instructed otherwise. If any section is inapplicable, write 'not applicable', 'none' or 'nil' to show you have not overlooked the section. You should also make copies of the completed forms.

4. Always use a pen or type on legal documents; never use pencil.

5. Do not cross out or erase anything you have written on your final forms.

6. You will find a helpful glossary of terms at the end of this **Law Pack** Guide. Refer to this glossary if you find unfamiliar terms.

7. Always keep legal documents in a safe place and in a location known to your spouse, family or solicitor.

Introduction

What is 'personal injury'?

'Personal injury' is the term used to cover all situations where someone seeks compensation from another who has caused him bodily injury. 'Injury' may be either physical or mental and in certain circumstances a personal injury claim can be on behalf of the victim of a fatal accident. A personal injury claimant could also claim for other sorts of loss, such as damage to personal possessions and financial loss, for example, loss of earnings. However, personal injury claims are distinctive in including a claim for compensation for pain and suffering and 'loss of amenity'. Invariably, a doctor (or other relevant medical practitioner) will be called as an expert to give an opinion about the injuries suffered.

Rather than being a distinct area of law, personal injury is really an area of the 'practice'. Personal injuries arise from many different situations and a claim may be worth many thousands of pounds, or less than £500. It may be a case involving two people (for example, two drivers involved in a road accident); or it may be a complex case involving large numbers of claimants against a company (industrial injuries) or hospital trust (clinical negligence). Claims may be brought in the High Court or a county court and may settle at an early stage before lawyers are involved, or be fought on to trial.

How to use this book

This book is designed for people without legal training. It is for those wishing to defend or bring their own claim; for those who want advice on whether or not to use a lawyer (and how to pay for one!); and for those simply wanting to know what to expect before they go to court.

This guide contains sections describing a brief overview of the law which might be relevant in a personal injury action: negligent driving, accidents at work, sporting injuries, assault, harassment and fatal accidents, to name but a few. There is advice on collecting evidence and preparing a case for court. In practice, most personal injury claims settle before trial, and there is a chapter on this very important aspect. Finally there is a detailed step-by-step guide on how to calculate the amount of damages.

Every chapter is designed to be useful for both the claimant and defendant; the aim is to give the reader the know-how to analyse his own case, *and* (which is as important) that of the 'other side'.

Note: In the interests of brevity and clarity I have chosen only to refer to 'his' and 'him'. As in Acts of Parliament and other authorities, the masculine is deemed to impart the feminine. This is a matter of style only, and in no way intended to offend.

I am grateful to Richard Menzies, barrister-at-law, for his permission to include the precedent on page 154.

Finally I would like to thank my husband Richard Wilson for his indefatigable help and support.

Felicity Mileham
The Chambers of Brian Higgs, QC, London

When is someone responsible?

In personal injury cases which go to court, the person (or company) who causes someone else to be injured may be ordered to pay the victim compensation for the injury itself, and for financial loss and costs arising from the injury. The 'claimant' (the person who has suffered the injury) must prove that the 'defendant' (the person or company said to have caused the personal injury) acted unlawfully. This does not mean necessarily that the defendant was committing a crime or acting 'illegally'. Instead, the claimant must prove that the defendant was either **negligent**, or in **breach of contract** or in **breach of a statutory duty** (defined below), or caused the injury by **assault** and **battery**, **harassment**, or **false imprisonment**. Each of these is known as a 'cause of action'. The claimant must also prove that the defendant's unlawful behaviour caused injury or financial loss. The court requires the claimant to mitigate (i.e. lessen) his losses as far as is reasonable (see page 138, 'The duty of the claimant to mitigate his loss').

Remember, however, that many personal injuries will not give rise to a legal claim. There will be no 'cause of action' where the accident occurred through no one's 'fault', or was caused by the claimant's own carelessness or deliberate action.

This chapter discusses various scenarios in which personal injury might arise. A brief description of the legal basis for a claim is given and selected sample 'Particulars of Claim' can be found in Appendix 1. The Particulars of Claim make up part of the Claim Form in which the claimant tells the story of the accident and details his injury and losses. The particulars can be included in the appropriate box on the Claim Form itself, or on a separate sheet of

---

Highlight

The claimant must prove that the defendant was either **negligent**, or in **breach of contract** or in **breach of a statutory duty**, or caused the injury by **assault** and **battery**, **harassment**, or **false imprisonment**. Each of these is known as a 'cause of action'.

---

paper enclosed with the Claim Form – see 'Claimant: issuing the Claim', page 89. The Particulars of Claim sets out all the elements of the 'cause of action' and carefully identifies the parties and facts relied on, including the injuries and losses.

Negligence

Negligence is a breach by the defendant of his duty to take care of the claimant's safety, which results in injury or loss. Only in certain circumstances will the law impose such a responsibility for the safety of others upon the citizen. Discussion on the types of situation where the defendant owes a 'duty of care' in respect of the claimant can be found later in this chapter.

Breach of contract

A claimant relying on 'breach of contract' must prove to a court that he had a contract with the defendant (such as an agreement to buy a product from him), that a term of the contract (such as a promise that the product is of satisfactory quality) has been breached and that the breach caused his injury and loss. Often the contract will be verbal, sometimes it will be written. Acts of Parliament may deem certain safety terms automatically included ('implied') into the contract.

Breach of statutory duty

Acts of Parliament have from time to time added to the list of causes of action available to claimants by creating 'statutory duties'. Of course, some duties imposed by an Act of Parliament or Regulations are designed to create criminal offences; damages are not directly available for breach of such duty. However, many other duties, if breached, create a 'civil liability', i.e. compensation by way of damages will be awarded by the courts. The claimant must be careful to bring the court's attention to the particular Statute or set of Regulations and prove that it applies to his case. He must then prove that the defendant has, by his action or inaction, breached the duty and that injury and loss has resulted.

Assault, battery, harassment and false imprisonment

These causes of action are characterised by the deliberate intent used by the defendant. They all involve one person directly

Highlight

Negligence is a breach by the defendant of his duty to take care of the claimant's safety, which results in injury or loss.

injuring another and are dealt with in detail under 'Injuries and stress caused to the victims of crime' on page 37.

Road traffic accidents

It is perhaps not surprising that a large proportion of personal injury litigation arises from road traffic accidents. Not only do road traffic accidents cause a great many injuries to road users, but also the existence of compulsory insurance against third party injury ensures that there is compensation money available to fight over. Road traffic accidents are generally based upon the law of negligence. It is well established that all road users owe a duty to take reasonable care to avoid injuring or causing damage to other road users. There are no absolute rules, such as the driver behind in a shunt accident being automatically in the wrong; the court will consider each case on its own merits.

Highlight

Road traffic accidents are generally based upon the law of negligence

Was the driver negligent?

Usually there will be a series of negligent actions that caused an accident. The claimant must analyse those actions of the other driver and particularise them in his Particulars of Claim. It is not enough to tell the court that the other driver merely failed to drive carefully in the circumstances. In any event, the defendant is entitled to know exactly what he is blamed for. The sample Particulars of Claim in Sample 1, Appendix 1 shows how detailed the analysis must be. Remember, the Particulars of Claim should succinctly tell the story of what happened and set out precisely why the defendant was negligent. For further help in filling in a Claim form see 'Claimant: issuing a claim', page 89.

Breach of the Highway Code

The Highway Code can be used by the courts to assess whether a motorist's standard of driving falls below the standard of care expected of road users. The claimant should bring to the court's attention any breach of the Highway Code where it contributed to or caused an accident.

Conviction for a driving offence

Where the other party to an accident has been convicted of an offence in connection with the accident, such as 'dangerous driving' (section 2, Road Traffic Act 1988) or 'careless or inconsiderate driving' (section 3, Road Traffic Act 1988) the conviction may be relied upon to prove negligence driving in a civil case. You will need to write to the court where the person was convicted (either a magistrates' or Crown court) asking for a 'certificate of conviction' for use in civil proceedings. Practice varies from court to court, so inquire by telephone to whom the letter should be addressed. The court will also be able to tell you what fee is payable. Your letter should include:

a)   the name of the convicted person;

b)   the date of the conviction (i.e. the day he pleaded guilty, or the day he was found guilty at trial);

c)   the offence involved.

A defendant facing a Particulars of Claim which contains details of a conviction may challenge the claimant in his Defence (see 'Defendant: how to deal with the Response Pack', page 93) on one of the following bases if appropriate:

a)   he was not convicted as alleged (i.e. he is not the person named in the certificate, or he was not convicted of the offence alleged, etc.);

b)   he was wrongly convicted, i.e. he did not commit the offence (note, however, that the civil court cannot overturn the conviction or sentence);

c)   although he was convicted as set down in the certificate, the conviction is not relevant to the issues in the civil case (for example, the illegal act did not cause the accident).

Mechanical faults

If a driver knows or ought to know that his vehicle has a mechanical fault which then causes or contributes to an accident he may, depending on the exact circumstances, be liable in negligence. He may also be liable under the Occupiers' Liability

Acts which apply to vehicles – see 'Accidents on (or in) private property', page 13.

Seatbelts or other compulsory or discretionary safety equipment

Highlight

A claimant who was not wearing a seatbelt or compulsory headgear at the time of the accident may be contributorily negligent

A claimant who was not wearing a seatbelt or compulsory headgear at the time of the accident may be contributorily negligent, in other words, the defendant may be able to prove that had the seatbelt been worn, the claimant would have reduced or avoided altogether the injuries. Damages will be reduced by a percentage reflecting the extent to which the court finds the claimant contributed to his injuries. For further discussion see under 'Contributory negligence', page 51.

Will the insurance company pay the damages?

A defendant motorist who is successfully sued for damages and costs arising out of a road traffic accident will want to call on his motor insurers to pay the money he owes the claimant. Normally, the defendant makes a claim on his insurance and the contract between him and his insurers will be sufficient to oblige the insurers to pay the sum. However, section 151 of the Road Traffic Act 1988 also obliges the insurer to pay the judgment sum (or part of it) in any situation where the insurance certificate has been issued except where (amongst other things):

a) the claimant, knowing that the defendant was driving a stolen vehicle, had allowed himself to become the defendant's passenger;

b) the claimant did not give the defendant's insurer notice that a claim had been brought against the defendant within seven days of the issue of the claim.

It is very important, therefore, the claimant writes a formal letter to confirm that a claim has been (or is being) issued; even if the insurer has been involved from the start and the 'pre-action protocol' (see page 83) has been complied with. See the sample letter overleaf.

Sample letter

Heather Cottage
Any Street
Anytown
AN1 1OW

Mega Motor Insurance Company
PO Box 34
Largetown

Dear Sir,

Your insured: Miss J Black
Accident date: 3rd October 2001
Your insured's vehicle: Peugeot 106 Registration G123 HIJ

[Further to my earlier correspondence] I write to inform you that I issued a claim against your Insured in the [Anytown County Court] on [date]. The Claim is for damages arising out of the negligent driving of your Insured. The Court has been asked to serve the relevant papers on [you/your solicitors] at [address].

This letter is intended to comply with the notice requirements of Section 152 of the Road Traffic Act 1988.

Yours faithfully,

Julian Green

Julian Green

If the insurers fail to pay the sum on the defendant's behalf, the claimant will have to bring a fresh claim against the insurer directly, invoking breach of the duty under the Road Traffic Act 1988 to pay.

Cases where the negligent driver cannot be traced

Under an agreement with the Government, the insurance industry, under the auspices of the Motor Insurers' Bureau (MIB), may pay compensation for people injured in hit-and-run-type accidents, where there is simply no one to name as defendant. The scheme does not apply to vehicles owned or in the possession of the Crown, or a local authority, police or health service bodies, unless those vehicles are being driven for unauthorised purposes at the time of the accident. The MIB will not pay compensation where the untraced driver deliberately used the vehicle as a weapon against the claimant. Nor will the MIB pay compensation to the claimant who allowed himself to become the defendant's passenger:

a) in a vehicle which he knew was stolen, or was being used to commit a crime, escape from lawful apprehension, etc;

b) knowing the defendant to be uninsured.

Instead of bringing a claim in the court, an application is made directly to the Motor Insurers' Bureau. Forms are available from the Motor Insurers' Bureau, 152 Silbury Boulevard, Central Milton Keynes, MK9 1NB. Applications must be made within three years of the accident. The claimant must have reported the accident to the police within 14 days of the accident, and co-operated with them in their investigations. As no court procedure is involved, the MIB will only pay up to £150 and VAT towards any legal fees incurred by the claimant.

Cases where the negligent driver is uninsured

A claimant who successfully sues a motorist for compensation may ask the Motor Insurers' Bureau to pay the judgment sum if it has not been paid in full within seven days after its due date. Although the agreement provides for the Bureau to make payments against any motorist the scheme has most application where the defendant was uninsured.

In circumstances where the negligent driver's insurance company cannot or will not pay, the Bureau will step into the breach and pay the full amount or the balance owing. To make a claim, however, the claimant should follow strictly the procedure set out below. Note that all documents must be faxed or sent by recorded/registered post (even hand-delivery or first class post will not be sufficient). The following checklist shows the steps that must be taken:

UNINSURED DRIVER CLAIMS

BEFORE THE CLAIM IS ISSUED

1) Write a letter stating that you have been injured in a road traffic accident as a result of the negligent driving of X who appears to be uninsured, giving details of the nature of the injuries, damages and losses. The letter should enclose any police report on the accident and a completed MIB Claim form (available from the Motor Insurers' Bureau, 152 Silbury Boulevard, Central Milton Keynes, MK9 1NB).

AFTER THE CLAIM HAS BEEN ISSUED

The claimant must give the following to the MIB:

2) Written notice that he has issued a claim against the defendant, enclosing a copy of the sealed (officially stamped) claim form, Particulars of Claim together with all the documents attached to it, copy of his motor insurance certificate and any correspondence between the claimant and defendant solicitors (if there is any) – within 14 days of issue of a claim (see page 89, 'Claimant: issuing a claim').

3) Written notice of the service of the proceedings on the defendant by the court – within seven days of receiving notice from the court that the proceedings have been served on the defendant claim (see page 89, 'Claimant: issuing a claim').

4) Written notice of the filing of a Defence by the defendant together with a copy of the Defence – within seven days of the filing of a Defence (see page 93, 'Defendant: how to deal with the Response Pack').

5) at least 35 days' notice in writing of the claimant's intention to ask the court for 'default judgment' (see page 95, 'Cutting litigation short; when can a trial be avoided?').

6) written notice of any amendments to statements of the case together with copies of the amended documents – within seven days of the amendments being agreed by the parties or authorised by the court.

7) written notice of the trial date – within seven days of it being given, or within seven days of the case being set down for trial.

AFTER THE DAMAGES HAVE BEEN AWARDED (OR AGREED)

8) The claimant must give to the MIB:

written notice that the defendant has not paid the judgment sum together with a copy of the sealed (officially stamped) court order and a request for payment by the MIB – within seven days of the sum becoming payable under the court order.

If the MIB do not pay the award, the claimant may bring a new claim naming the Motor Insurers' Bureau as defendant.

Accidents involving buses

Where a bus driver has driven negligently and caused personal injuries the bus company can be sued on the principle that it is 'vicariously liable' for its employee, the bus driver. The person injured may have been another road user (driver or pedestrian), or a passenger on the bus. In situations where the claimant was a road user the usual rules apply (see above). Where the claimant was a passenger the bus company must additionally comply with certain 'statutory duties' under the Public Service Vehicles (Conduct of Drivers, Inspectors, Conductors, and Passengers) Regulations 1990 (as amended). Therefore, passengers injured on buses may rely on two causes of action: negligence and breach of statutory duty. Failure to take reasonable care for the safety of passengers is the basis for a claim in negligence. Bus drivers and conductors must also take all reasonable precautions to ensure the safety of passengers who are entering, leaving or already on the vehicle. Failure to do so will form the basis of a claim of breach of statutory duty. It may be that the bus company's employees' behaviour is both negligent and a breach of the statutory duty. A sample Particulars of Claim is included at Sample 3, Appendix 1.

Accidents in public places ▬▬▬▬▬▬

'Public area' is not a legal term. It is a collective description of any land or premises over which the public has a right to use or pass over for general or specific purposes. Thus it includes highways and land over which there is a public right of way. Often a premises to which the public has ready access, such as a car park, or leisure facility is actually privately owned, which the public may use due to a contract with the owner, or by invitation only. For accidents occurring on these privately owned areas, see generally 'Accidents on (or in) private property'.

There are numerous causes of accidents which might happen in a public space. The most frequently occurring are the 'tripping and slipping' accidents. The condition of the area due to poor maintenance or bad construction might lead to hazards: uneven paving stones, holes in tarmac, uncovered manholes, dangerous steps, slippery areas, poor street lighting and damaged fencing, to name but a few. Similarly, hazards may have been created as a result of works carried out by various authorities or contractors. These might include objects such as bollards left in the way of passers-by, inadequate warnings of hazards or unguarded works. Other accidents might occur because of falling or projecting objects from buildings structures or land next to or surrounded by the public area.

There are potentially two causes of action: negligence, and breach of statutory duty. The first task is to identify the probable defendant. Liability for the state of the road or other public area will probably be that of the relevant highway authority (usually the local authority). In cases where water, gas, electricity or communications companies have been digging up roads to undertake works on pipes beneath the surface they may be liable for dangerous objects on or condition of the highway.

Liability for the condition of the highway

There is duty of care imposed on highway authorities by section 41 of the Highways Act 1980 to maintain the roads in their care. Under the Act, the duty to maintain includes the duty to repair. There is much case law on the subject, and judges have frequently commented that each case must be looked at individually. For example, there is no rule of law stating that an authority is negligent if paving stones project above the surface by a particular amount; there is no magic number. The court will consider each time whether the situation posed a danger to the public which the highway authority should have remedied or prevented. It is certain, however, that the courts will not impose on highway authorities the duty to keep the roads and pavements in 'bowling green' condition (in the words of Lord Justice Dillon). Would a reasonable person look at the 'hazard' as 'presenting a real source of danger'? There is a statutory defence available to the highway authority, under section 58 of the Highways Act 1980, that the authority took reasonable care to ensure that the relevant part of the highway was 'not dangerous' to persons using the highway. In considering whether the authority has proved the defence, the court will consider the character of the highway and the traffic expected to use it, the standard of maintenance appropriate for the highway given its character and the expected traffic, the state of repair the reasonable person would expect, whether the highway authority knew or could have been expected to know of the danger posed by the condition of the highway, and whether (where the authority could not reasonably be expected to have repaired the highway before the accident happened) any warning signs had been displayed. Of course other defences may also be relevant (see chapter 2). For sample Particulars of Claim in cases against the highway authority, see Sample 4, Appendix 1.

Road works and disrepair caused by utility companies and their contractors

Although the New Works and Street Works Act 1991 and the Public Utilities Street Works Act 1950 lay down requirements (including safety measures) as to how work, repairs, etc. must be undertaken, no claim for damages arises directly from the failure to comply with these provisions. The Acts instead impose criminal liability on persons (or companies) failing to comply with the requirements. However, the failure may in itself be a measure of the negligence (i.e. a breach of the duty under the common law to take care for road users). The Acts provide that the person liable to repair the street known as the 'street authority' (usually the highway authority but sometimes another person known in the 1991 Act as a 'street manager') must keep records of current and future works in the street which may be inspected free of charge. The safety requirements are set out in Section 66 of the 1991 Act and usually apply to the street authority or someone acting under a street works licence from street authority.

Road works

The person undertaking works on the street must ensure that areas of the street that are broken up, or on which equipment or materials are deposited, are adequately guarded and lit. Where reasonable, signs giving guidance or direction (i.e. around the dangerous area) should be placed and maintained by the person doing the works. In ensuring these measures, the person doing the works must consider the needs of people with a disability.

Reinstatement of the road

The person undertaking road works has a duty under section 70 of the 1991 Act to 'reinstate' the road. Thus he must fill in holes he has made, remove equipment and materials, replace street furniture and other safety features. Under section 71 he must also comply with Codes of Practice made by the Minster of Transport setting out the specification of materials to be used and performance standards.

Liability for other accidents in public areas

A person may be injured by a danger existing on land adjoining public areas. This might be because of activities on private land (such as stray golf balls from a driving range raining down on users of a road running next to golf club land), or it may be due to the state of the land or structures on it (such as signposts falling off buildings or trees falling onto the highway). In both cases it may be possible to prove that the defendant's behaviour was 'negligent'. In other words, that he owed a duty to take reasonable care for the safety of the claimant, that he failed to fulfil that duty,

Highlight

The person undertaking works on the street must ensure that areas of the street that are broken up, or on which equipment or materials are deposited, are adequately guarded and lit.

whether by action or inaction, and that as a consequence the claimant was injured.

Where the object that caused the damage was 'artificial' (for example, a signpost or lamp) among the defences available to the defendant is that the dangerous condition or situation was caused by a trespasser or by 'unobservable operation of nature' (i.e. a natural process which is largely invisible to the onlooker). The rule is slightly different where natural objects pose a danger, such as trees. In respect of such things the landowner (or other person in control) has a duty to take reasonable care for the safety of people using adjacent public land to the extent that he knew, or ought to have known, that the condition or placement of the tree in question was dangerous to such people.

Accidents on (or in) private property

'Private property' is not a legal term. It is used here to describe property belonging to or leased by an individual or company over which the public has no general right of entry. Members of the public may be invited or allowed to enter for general specific purposes (such as shoppers entering a shop, or postmen walking up the garden path to deliver a letter). Alternatively, the right of entry might arise from a contract between the owner and visitor. People who enter or do things that exceed the permission or terms of their visit, or those who were never allowed to be there in the first place, are known as 'trespassers'.

This section discusses the situations in which occupiers of private property may be sued for personal injuries caused by the state or condition of the property, rather than accidents directly caused by the actions (or omissions) of people.

Example 1

I am travelling as a passenger in my friend Danny's car. He collides with a stationary vehicle, and I am injured. In my claim for damages Danny will be the defendant. The cause of action will be negligence – the court will only be considering the way he drove.

(See further at page 3, 'Road traffic accidents')

Example 2

I am travelling as a passenger in my friend Danny's car. Whilst we are driving along the front passenger seat shoots forward without warning and I am injured as a result. I bring a claim against Danny for damages. The cause of action is negligence and breach of statutory duty under the Occupiers' Liability Act. The manner in which he drove is not relevant; the court will instead be concerned with the safety of the seat and whether or not he knew about its dangerous condition, etc; in other words the duty of care placed on the owner of private property – in this instance, the car.

(See below, 'Occupiers' liability')

Negligence

The case law which has built up over the years setting down the duties of property owners to lawful visitors is complex. Some legal commentators consider that negligence as a cause of action has effectively been superseded by the onset of the Occupiers' Liability Acts 1957 and 1984. As a result, although negligence is often stated as a cause of action in addition to occupiers' liability under either of the Acts (see below), in reality the usual focus of the court will be on the latter. The advantage of relying on both causes of action is that it adopts what lawyers call a 'belt and braces approach'. If, for whatever reason, one cause of action fails, the other may survive. Once the claimant has proved unlawful behaviour on the part of the defendant (whether by negligence or breach of a statutory common duty), he will obtain damages for his loss. It does not matter, as it were, the nature of that unlawful behaviour.

Negligence is particularly important where for one reason or another the Occupiers' Liability Acts or the legislation relating to landlords do not apply (see below). In a claim on the basis of negligence, the claimant must prove (a) that the defendant owed him a duty in the circumstances, to avoid foreseeable accidents, (b) that the duty was breached (i.e. through the defendant's carelessness the accident happened) and (c) as a result, injury and loss occurred.

Highlight

The case law which has built up over the years setting down the duties of property owners to lawful visitors is complex.

Scenarios that might give rise to negligence claims may include injuries caused to passers-by or to those on adjacent land or roads, by dangerous activities on land or the dangerous condition of land, buildings, structures, vessels or vehicles. Workmen have a duty to take reasonable care for the safety of those they know or ought to know (or should know) may be affected by the works.

The responsibility of the occupiers of property to lawful visitors

All occupiers of property have a duty to take reasonable care that visitors (the duty to trespassers is dealt with below) will be reasonably safe using the premises (Occupiers' Liability Act 1957). What is 'reasonable care' will depend on all the circumstances of the case. The law therefore does not expect the occupier to ensure the absolute safety of the visitor, even supposing that were ever possible.

Along with the usual defences (see chapter 2, Defences) available to the occupier the following are effectively defences under the Act:

a) that the warning he gave the visitor (by notice or verbally) of the danger was enough to enable the visitor to be reasonably safe; or

b) (where the constructing, maintenance or repair contractors caused the danger) that he was reasonable in employing contractors, that he took steps to ensure the contractors were reasonably competent and took steps to ensure that the work was properly done.

Identifying the defendant; who is an occupier?

To qualify as an occupier under the Act, the defendant must be someone who has direct and sufficient control or supervision of the property. This might be the owner or tenant or other occupier of the land, vehicle, etc. The occupier may be a person or a company (see page 73, 'Whom to sue?'). More than one person or company may have sufficient control and supervision to qualify as occupier at any one time. Occupiers are 'vicariously liable' for the unlawful actions of their employees and can be sued as defendant where the employees have failed to fulfil their duty under the Act.

The defendant and claimant may be in a relationship additional to that of property owner and visitor; they might be employer/ employee, school/pupil, parties to a contract, hospital/patient, shop owner/ shopper, etc. The relationship does not alter the duty and in some situations there might be other causes of action (such as breach of contract).

Types of property subject to the Occupiers' Liability Act

The duties in the Act cover various types of property, such as land, vehicles, vessels and aircraft which may be fixed or moveable. Structures found on land, such as buildings, scaffolding, wells, ladders, paths and walls are also included, and where they pose an unlawful danger to visitors the 'occupier' will be held liable.

The duty occupiers owe to trespassers and lawful users of private rights of way

The Occupiers' Liability Act 1984 imposes a more limited duty on occupiers of property towards trespassers, other uninvited visitors and to those who own a private right of way over someone else's land (sometimes known as a 'right of access'). Broadly, the Act lays down that an occupier take reasonable care that such people do not suffer injury from any dangers he is aware of posed by his property. The claimant trespasser must prove that the type of danger is one that the defendant occupier should reasonably have offered him protection from in all the circumstances. It is a defence for the defendant to prove that he took reasonable steps in the circumstances to give warnings of the danger or to discourage people from risking the danger.

Children

The Act takes into account the fact that children who trespass onto property are likely to be less careful for their own safety than adults are. Thus landowners and other occupiers of land (including buildings) must take reasonable care that the property is in such a condition that it does not pose a danger to children who stray on to it. It is well to remember, however, that children should be supervised appropriately by their parents or other adults 'in loco parentis'. It may be that a child has trespassed because of inadequate supervision and in that case the defendant might be able to prove that the child's parents are liable wholly or in part for his injuries.

Identifying the defendant; who is an occupier?

To qualify as an occupier under the Act, the defendant must be someone who has direct and sufficient control or supervision of the property. This might by the owner or tenant or other occupier of the land, vehicle, etc. The occupier may be a person or a company (see page 73, 'Whom to sue?'). More than one person or company may have sufficient control and supervision to qualify as occupier at any one time. Occupiers are 'vicariously liable' for the unlawful actions of their employees and can be sued as defendant where the employees have failed to fulfil their duty under the Act.

Highlight

Occupiers are 'vicariously liable' for the unlawful actions of their employees

Types of property subject to the Occupiers' Liability Act 1984

The duties in the Act cover various types of property, such as land, vehicles, vessels and aircraft and may be fixed or moveable. Structures found on land, such as buildings, scaffolding, wells, ladders, paths and walls are also included, and where they pose an unlawful danger to visitors the 'occupier' will be held liable.

Landlords' responsibility to their tenants for defective premises

In some circumstances, a landlord may be liable for defects on the property rented out which cause personal injury to their tenants (and in some cases to others, lawfully at the property). The starting point is the landlord-tenant relationship. Where a mere 'licence' to occupy property has been granted, no lease will exist and the parties are in a legal relationship of licensor and licensee. Most arrangements relating to residential property create a lease (whether oral or written). Thus a relationship of landlord and tenant is created. The landlord's duty in relation to hazards on the property or to the condition of the property depends on whether the defects arose due to his own positive actions, and whether the defects occurred before the lease was created or whilst the tenant was *in situ*.

Property defective prior to lease

One of the effects of Section 3 of the Defective Premises Act 1972 is that the tenant may claim damages from his landlord for injuries caused by negligent construction, repair, maintenance or demolition work done by the landlord or his employers before the tenancy began.

Defects that arise during the letting

Section 4 of the Defective Premises Act 1972 provides that the landlord has a duty of care in respect of defects on the premises in limited circumstances. To succeed in a claim under this section, the claimant tenant must prove that the landlord:

a) is obliged to repair the particular defect by the lease itself, or by terms imposed on the agreement by statute (see below); or

b) the lease (whether oral or written) gives the landlord the right to enter the rented premises in order to carry out maintenance or repair work.

It goes without saying that the tenant will have no claim for personal injuries caused by disrepair or defects for which, under the lease, he is responsible. Under section 4 of the Defective Premises Act 1972 (in addition to any other duty to repair the defect), the landlord must take such care as is reasonable in all the circumstances to make all those who might reasonably be expected to be affected by the disrepair (including the tenant, his visitors and even people outside the property) reasonably safe.

As mentioned above, the statutory duty only arises in certain situations. To determine whether the conditions are met, the claimant-tenant must first establish what duties the landlord has under the lease. The second criterion (that the landlord has permission to enter the property to undertake repairs and maintenance) is easy to establish with a quick look at the lease. The first criterion (that the landlord is responsible for specific repairs or maintenance) is found either expressly in the wording of the lease, or is imposed on (or 'implied' into) some leases by statute. The landlord and tenant agree between them when the lease is granted (verbally or in writing) who is responsible for the various repairs. If nothing has been agreed as to repairs, the general rule is that the tenant is fully responsible for the state of the property. The exception to this rule is created by section 11 of the Landlord and Tenant Act 1985. It applies only to residential

Highlight

To determine whether the conditions are met, the claimant-tenant must first establish what duties the landlord has under the lease.

premises (dwelling houses) leased for a term of less than seven years. By section 11, the landlord is responsible for keeping the following in repair and proper working order:

a) the structure and exterior of the dwelling house, including drains gutters and external pipes;

b) installations in the rented premises that supply water, gas, electricity and sanitation, such as basins, sinks, baths, lavatories, supply pipes, etc. – but not the 'appliances' which use the supplies, such as cookers, fridges and washing machines;

c) installations in the rented premises that heat water or space – such as the central heating system and hot water tank.

The section only obliges the landlord to repair the installations where their disrepair affects the enjoyment (which means use rather than pleasure) of the property. Similarly, the section does not oblige the landlord to instal such installations where they did not exist at the time the lease was agreed. The tenant is also expected to look after the premises in a 'tenant-like manner'. It is not surprising that the landlord is not liable to repair installations that have been damaged by the tenant's wilful or negligent behaviour.

Accidents and other injuries in the workplace

Accidents which can occur at work, or symptoms that are brought on by tasks performed at work, are many and varied. In order to obtain compensation an employee must prove that the injury was caused by the negligence, breach of statutory duty or breach of contract by the employer. These different causes of action arise from the employer's duty towards the employee.

The law of negligence imposes upon an employer a duty to provide the following for each employee:

(1) safe premises;

(2) safe machinery and other equipment;

(3) properly skilled workers to superintend the business;

(4) a 'safe system of work' – this means the rules and procedures used by the employer to organise the work of the employees: incorporating safety precautions, the number of men/women to be employed, the roles to be taken by the employees and the provision of necessary supervision.

Additionally, employers are subject to the various statutes and regulations that govern health and safety for their employees. It is essential to refer the court to the correct regulations. Some types of employment, such as that on oilrigs and sea-going ships, have their own regulations, and the general Health and Safety Regulations mentioned below may not apply. Additionally, not every breach of a statutory duty will give rise to a 'cause of action'; some statutory duties give rise to criminal offences rather than civil liability. It is impossible in a guide such as this to give more than a brief overview of the most frequent types of claim.

Evidence

The claimant must be absolutely clear as to how the accident was caused when he considers whether the employer is to blame. It will usually be necessary, except in the simplest cases, to obtain expert evidence from a safety officer, qualified engineer with the relevant experience or other appropriate professional at an early stage. The employee must be able to prove by expert evidence that his injury and loss was caused by the conditions or hazard in question at his work. If he relies on negligence or some other statutory causes of action of action the claimant must also prove (inevitably by expert evidence) that the defendant was at fault (i.e. that he has done something wrong or omitted to do something he ought to have done).

Accidents caused by co-employees

In taking reasonable steps to avoid risks to his employees, the employer must select properly skilled people to manage and superintend the business. In other words, the employer has a duty to employees (whilst they are acting in the course of their employment) to provide 'safe' co-employees. This is partly because of his common law duty of care to employees and is governed by the law of negligence. The employer cannot

Highlight

In taking reasonable steps to avoid risks to his employees, the employer must select properly skilled people to manage and superintend the business.

discharge his obligation merely by delegating responsibility for the safety of employees to an employee or a subcontractor. However, not all accidents at work will be laid at the door of the employer. The employer need only take steps that are 'reasonable' in all the circumstances to avoid risks. Matters such as the training, specific and general orders, discipline and the record and personality of the co-employee, as well as the particular needs and circumstances of the injured employee, may all be relevant.

Accidents caused by dangerous conditions of the workplace

An employer owes a duty to each employee to provide and maintain a reasonably safe workplace (including access ways). Whether the employee has taken reasonable steps to avoid dangers and risks is a matter of fact in each case. The court will take into account any safety precautions taken; what caused the hazard; whether the hazard is long-standing; whether the hazard was temporary or transitory; the extent to which the employer knew about the hazard; the particular needs and circumstances of the injured employee. Other factors may also be relevant in a particular situation. It may be that the dangerous condition is caused by an unsafe system of work (see above), and the employer might be liable for this. The system of work must not only exist on paper or in the minds of supervisors; it must also be implemented.

The Workplace (Health, Safety and Welfare) Regulations 1992, which were brought in under powers conferred by the Health and Safety at Work Act 1974, set standards for ventilation, indoor temperature, lighting, cleanliness and disposal of waste materials, room dimensions and space, workstations and seating, the condition of flooring, the prevention of falling objects, windows, the circulation of pedestrians and vehicles, doors and gates, escalators, sanitary conveniences, washing facilities, drinking water, restrooms and other facilities. Most of the duties are not absolute and are often subject to a qualification such as 'as far as reasonably practicable'.

Accidents caused by the nature of the work

Injuries caused by the way a task is carried out may be the result of the employer's failure to provide a safe system of work, or lack of adequate training and supervision. If the employer has failed in these duties towards his employees – and the failure has resulted in the injury – then he may well have been negligent.

Heavy lifting jobs are covered by the Manual Handling Operations Regulations 1992 which were brought in under powers conferred by the Health and Safety at Work Act 1974. Manual handling means 'transporting or supporting a load (including lifting, putting down, pushing, pulling, carrying or moving it)'. Under regulation 4, the employer:

a) must avoid, as far as 'reasonably practicable', the need for an employee to undertake any manual handling which involves the risk of injuring him;

b) or (where it is necessary for the employee to undertake manual handling), the employer must assess the risk of the manual handling task in question and take appropriate steps to reduce the risks to the lowest reasonably practicable level (by introducing a safe system of work), and indicate to the employee at least generally or specifically the weight of each load, and the heaviest side of a load which does not have a central centre of gravity.

The regulations also require the employee to make full and proper use of the 'system of work' instituted by the employer. A failure by the employee to follow any orders or protocol that are part of that system of work may result in him not being successful in his breach of statutory duty claim if he gets injured. Alternatively, he may be held to be 'contributorily negligent' (see 'Contributory negligence', page 51).

Personal injuries caused by work equipment

Defective machinery

There is a common law duty for the owner or supplier of appliances or equipment to take reasonable care to see that the equipment is fit and safe for the purpose for which is to be used. Thus all employers or anyone else who supplies defective equipment to an employee may be liable in negligence under this common law rule. Additionally an injured employee can rely on section 1(1) of the Employers' Liability (Defective Equipment) Act 1969. To succeed, he must prove that the injury was caused in the course of his employment by defective equipment provided by the employer for the purposes of the employer's business (i.e. to use at work). The employer is liable even if the defect is the fault of someone else (a third party) – whether a manufacturer, another employee or an independent contractor.

Further duties are imposed on employers in respect of the safety of work equipment by various regulations. The main provisions, which apply to most employers and the self-employed, can be summarised as follows. Employers must:

1   ensure that equipment is suitable for the purpose for which it is intended;

2   ensure that equipment is maintained in an efficient state, in efficient working order and in good repair;

3   ensure that equipment posing a specific risk to health or safety must only be used by the employee given the task of using (or modifying, repairing maintaining or servicing) the equipment, and adequate training must be provided for such employees;

4   provide all employees who are using equipment with adequate health and safety information and training and where appropriate, written instructions relating to the use of the equipment (the information and instructions must be readily comprehensible);

5   provide fixed guards and other protection devices as appropriate to prevent access to any dangerous part of machinery or to stop the movement of any dangerous part of machinery before a person enters the danger zone; the fixed guards or protection devices themselves must be suitable for the purpose, be well-built of sound materials and must not themselves pose a risk to health and safety, etc.

For the actual wording of the regulations, and for further employers' duties, please refer to The Provision and Use of Work Equipment Regulations 1992.

Accidents at work involving machinery or other equipment may be caused by various factors. The equipment might be unsuitable for the purpose for which it is used; it may suffer from a design fault; it may be defective when new, or become defective at a later date; or poor maintenance may result in hazards.

Injuries caused by using equipment

There are various situations in which workers may suffer personal injury from using equipment that is not in itself defective or obviously hazardous. Some, such as computer screens or headsets have received media interest. Others are generally well known in particular industries. Apart from the common law duty of employers to provide a safe system of work, regulations may impose other duties on employers. The Health and Safety (Display Screen Equipment) Regulations 1992 are an example. These require employers (amongst other things) to provide breaks or other interruptions for employees working at screens, regular eye and eyesight tests for certain employees (as well as providing them with the appropriate spectacles or other corrective equipment where appropriate) and, for certain employees, health and safety training and information about the health and safety aspects of working at a work station.

Accidents caused by the absence or inadequacy of protective gear

An employer's duty to take reasonable steps to avoid risks to its employees may, in the particular circumstances require him to provide protective equipment such as goggles, gloves, clothing, etc. A failure to do so may therefore be negligence. The Personal Protective Equipment at Work Regulations 1992 stipulates that the employer must 'ensure that suitable personal protective equipment is provided to his employees who may be exposed to a risk to their health and safety while at work except where and to the extent that such a risk has been adequately controlled by other means which are equally or more effective' (regulation 4(1)). There are provisions in the regulations for determining what is meant by 'suitable' and requirements that employers assess the risks properly, that protective equipment is maintained and replaced where appropriate, that training is provided and use of the equipment is enforced.

Defective products

Where a product or item causes injury and other loss to someone coming into contact with it there may be a liability. The term 'product' covers various different items, not only manufactured goods, but also foodstuffs, minerals, substances and even electricity, water, etc. Although lawyers talk of 'defective products' they use the term to cover not only items that malfunction, but also those that have design faults, and those that are provided with inadequate or no warnings, or misleading instructions. Many products are sold precisely because of hazardous qualities that make them useful in everyday life, for example a knife or rat poison. We would not say they were 'defective' merely because they posed a danger to people who might come into contact with them.

There are various 'causes of action' open to the person injured by a defective product. The defect or other fault may be caused by someone's negligence, or the 'producer' of the product may be liable under the Consumer Protection Act 1987, or other legislation. If the item was purchased by the person injured, the seller may be in breach of contract. It is quite common for a claimant to rely on more than one cause of action in order to maximise his chance of success and the amount of damages recoverable. Similarly, the claimant may have causes of action against more than one person, in which case it is sensible to name each as a defendant to the action. It is important to set out carefully the different complaints against each defendant in the Particulars of Claim.

Negligence

The claimant must prove that the defendant was the person responsible for the 'defect' or other fault. Various types of defendant have been held to have been liable, including manufacturers, assemblers and repairers of malfunctioning products, installers, distributors, wholesalers and retailers who have (in the way they have dealt with, handled or stored the item) caused it to be dangerous, or who have not provided the necessary safety information, etc.

It is important for the claimant to examine the route the product has taken, because the correct defendant (or defendants) must be named and his precise failing identified. For example, where a part is defective and incorporated into an otherwise perfectly good product, the maker of the part may be liable to the claimant for negligently making the defective part, and the manufacturer of the finished product may be liable to the claimant for failing to check the overall safety of the product, or for failing to use reputable suppliers. Thus, there may be more that one defendant and if the claimant is successful against more than one of them, the court may apportion the damages payable by each to him.

The defendant will be vicariously liable for the negligence of his employees (see 'Suing an individual's employer', page 74), but not for sub-contractors employed by him. If sub-contractors have been negligent, they may be sued directly. If the main contractor is negligent in his own right (by failing to hire reputable contractors, or failing to supervise work properly, for example) he may also be sued.

The courts will take into account all the surrounding circumstances on the issue of the safety (or otherwise) of a product. This may include any relevant British Standard guidelines (also known as the kitemark system) or other non-statutory safety standards. Even though such guidelines are not mandatory, they provide a guide to what is considered a safe standard for products.

Normally, the claimant must call evidence to prove how the defendant failed to fulfil his duty owed to the claimant. This will usually involve calling an expert witness (see 'Expert evidence', page 108). On rare occasions there may be no proof as to exactly what went wrong, except the simple fact that the product caused the injury. The claimant in such circumstances may ask the court to infer from the evidence of the accident and the injury that the only probable explanation for the events is that the defendant was negligent because the defect should not normally have occurred, and that the item in question was always only in the control of the defendant. This rule of evidence is known by its Latin tag: *res ipsa loquitur* (meaning 'the thing speaks for itself'). Clearly, if there is evidence of the defendant's negligence causing the fault, there is no need to rely on this principle.

If the claimant is successful, he may recover damages to compensate for injury and damage to property, including the losses and expenses arising from the injury and damage (see chapter 5, 'How compensation is calculated'). In this cause of action (unlike an action for breach of contract), there is no recovery of the value of the product that was defective.

Example

Narinda is given a new car by her parents for her 18th birthday. When she takes it for a run, the exhaust explodes, injuring her and damaging the car and her laptop computer, which was in the boot.

As Narinda did not purchase the car, she cannot bring a claim in breach of contract. She can, however, claim against the negligent defendants. If successful, she will receive compensation (damages) for her pain suffering and loss of amenity; the losses arising from her injuries (such as loss of earnings); and the extra costs caused by her injuries (such as medical bills, and adapting her home). Narinda will also be able to obtain compensation for the damage caused to her property such as the laptop and the clothes she was wearing. However, under the rules of negligence she will not be compensated for damage to her car.

Consumer Protection Act 1987

This Act was brought in as a result of a European Union Directive on consumer protection; other European Union countries are similarly obliged to enact the Directive.

Claims under the Act are based on the principle that a claimant suffered injury or property damage caused by a defect in a product, or by a part contained in a product. In many cases, the defendant may have also been negligent (see above) or in breach of contract (see below under 'Breach of contract'). If so, it is wise to frame the claim on more than one cause of action to maximise chances of success. However, in a few cases the Act may provide the only cause of action available to a claimant. For example, where the defendant is someone who, although responsible for producing or importing or supplying the product, did not owe a 'duty of care' towards that particular claimant; or if he did owe a such a duty to the claimant, he did not in fact breach the duty by being 'careless', the claimant will not succeed in negligence, but may do so under the Act.

The claimant must satisfy the court that the thing causing the injury is a 'product' within the meaning of the Act. He must also satisfy the court that the product was 'defective' within the meaning of the Act. Finally he must prove that the defendant belongs to one of the four classes of people who will be held responsible under the Act.

What counts as a product?

Goods (including substances, food, drugs, aircraft, vehicles and ships) and electricity are all 'products' under the Act. It does not matter if the defective item is a raw material or a part used as a component in the finished article. Agricultural produce and fish that have undergone an 'industrial process' (such as canning, or cooking) also count as 'goods' within the meaning of the Act.

What is a 'defect'?

An item which falls below the standard of safety that people are generally entitled to expect is defective within the meaning of the Act. The item in question may be defective because it malfunctions. Where a product is of necessity inherently hazardous (such as a kettle or rat poison) it will not be defective by virtue of its dangerous qualities. However, it may be defective where the instructions or information accompanying the product are inadequate to warn the user against misuse or misadventure.

Who can be sued under the Act?

Most manufactured, extracted and supplied goods pass through many hands before reaching the consumer. The Act defines who may be sued for defects, some of whom might not be directly responsible for the condition of the product. The four classes of people or companies who may be sued under the Act are 'producers', 'rebranders' (my term), 'importers' and 'suppliers'.

- • 'Producers' include the manufacturer of the product, the abstractor or excavator of the product (such as mining companies or oil extractors) or the processor of produce (on an industrial sale).

- 'Rebranders' are people or companies who add their name, trade mark or other label to a product manufactured, processed or abstracted by someone else, so that to the consumer it seems that the rebrander was in fact the producer. Supermarket own-brand goods made under contract by an unidentified supplier come under this category.

- 'Importers' are narrowly defined as those who import the defective product in question from outside the European Union into a member state (even if that is not the UK).

- 'Suppliers' are defined as any person who supplies (by selling, hiring, giving, etc.) the defective product in the course of his business to someone else. The supply in question need not be made to the injured person; the definition includes all the people or companies involved in the supply chain. However, suppliers may only be sued if, having been asked by the injured person to identify the producers, rebranders or importers within a reasonable time of the injury occurring, they fail to identify those people, or even to identify the person who supplied the product.

Claims under the Act

It is possible for the claimant to sue more than one defendant for damages resulting from a defective product. If two or more defendants are found to be liable (or admit liability), the court may apportion the amount of damages each must pay to the claimant under the Civil Liabilities (Contribution) Act 1978. Similarly, if the claimant has contributed to the risk of injury by his own negligence ('contributory negligence') the court may reduce the amount of damages he is awarded proportionately.

Damages may be claimed for personal injury or death. Compensation for property worth more than £275 damaged by the defective product (after subtracting the relevant amounts for 'contributory negligence' by the claimant and interest) may also be awarded under the Act. It is not possible to obtain compensation for the cost of or damage to the defective product itself.

Other statutory causes of action

An employer's responsibility for the safety of work equipment has been discussed earlier under 'Personal injuries caused by work equipment'. There are other Acts of Parliament dealing with specific areas of safety, such as the Vaccine Damage Payments Act 1979; however, such regimes are outside the scope of this guide.

Breach of contract

Where someone sells, or hires an item to a consumer, a contract is formed. Similarly, where a person undertakes a job of work for a consumer and provides goods as part of the work (such as the installation of a new kitchen, or the building of a swimming pool), a contract for the supply of goods and services has been formed. Where the seller or hirer is acting in the course of his business, various Acts of Parliament insert terms as to the quality of goods into the contract. For example, the item or goods sold, hired or supplied must be of 'satisfactory quality', they must be fit for the purpose which the consumer told the seller he intended to use them (if he had done so) and they must match the description under which they were sold (or supplied or hired). The relevant provisions are sections 13 and 14 of the Sale of Goods Act 1979; section 10 of the Supply of Goods (Implied Terms) Act 1973; and sections 4 and 9 of the Supply of Goods and Services Act 1982.

The claimant must prove that there was a contract with the defendant by which he acquired the defective product. He must demonstrate what the terms of the contract were, by reference to express promises as to safety or terms inserted by an Act of Parliament, and prove that one or more terms of the contract were breached. The claimant finally must prove that the breach of contract caused his injury, damage to his property and other financial loss (such as loss of profit). Unlike claims based on negligence or the Consumer Protection Act (see above), it is possible to obtain compensation for damage to the defective product itself in a claim based on breach of contract.

Clinical negligence and other healthcare issues

Clinical negligence is a branch of the law of negligence which sets down the duty of care that a healthcare professional (doctor, anaesthetist, dentist, pathologist, etc.) has towards patients in his care. The other cause of action frequently found in claims that arise in a clinical situation is battery (often described as an assault), where a healthcare professional has physically touched the body of a patient (either to give treatment or inappropriately) and in so doing has exceeded any consent the patient may have given. The area is continually developing and case law is important for setting down parameters of the duty owed by healthcare professionals.

Negligence

A healthcare professional has a duty to 'exercise reasonable skill and care' in treating a patient. A hospital has a similar duty to ensure its employees exercise reasonable skill and care in the treatment and care of patients it has admitted, or treated in Accident and Emergency or as an outpatient. When assessing whether the defendant professional or hospital has been negligent, the court will look carefully at the mistake made. There may have been a misdiagnosis, wrongful treatment, poorly executed procedure, poor nursing standards or other failure to take care of the patient's health. The court will ask itself the question, 'Has the professional shown the ordinary skill and care expected of a competent professional in the same field in his treatment or care of the patient?' In other words, the healthcare professional will be judged by the standard of his peers. The law does not expect health workers to perform miracles. Normally a healthcare worker in the same field as the defendant will be called as an expert witness to help the court assess whether the defendant's actions were competent. Where a procedure or treatment divides medical opinion, the law will not criticise and hold liable a healthcare professional for using a controversial method, as long as that method is recognised by a respectable body of medical opinion.

Highlight

The area is continually developing and case law is important for setting down parameters of the duty owed by healthcare professionals.

Battery

Many medical procedures, from operations to nursing care, involve the use of physical contact between a healthcare professional or health worker and the patient. If done without the consent of the patient, the physical contact would amount to a 'battery' (see 'Assault and battery', page 39). In some circumstances it may be appropriate for written consent (by signing a form) to be given; in other circumstances verbal consent will suffice. The most important thing is that consent is 'informed'. Consent obtained by fraud or misrepresentation on the part of the healthcare professional is not valid. Parents may give their consent to examinations and procedures on young children; however, children who have enough understanding and maturity may give consent for themselves. Healthcare workers who perform a physical act which is above and beyond, or outside the scope of the consent given by the patient may have committed a battery, and damages may be recoverable for injuries caused by the 'unauthorised' procedure. However, doctors and other professionals do not need consent from an unconscious patient where a procedure is 'necessary' to preserve life or health.

National Health Service care

The principles set out above apply to medical professionals within the NHS. Health authorities or partnerships that employ nurses, doctors, surgeons and other healthcare professionals (even 'agency' workers) are 'vicariously liable' for their employees' wrongful actions (see page 74, 'Suing an individual's employer' and page 77, 'Claims against firms or other partnerships'). Doctors who are not 'employed' can be sued directly.

Private healthcare

The principles set out above also apply to medical care undertaken privately. Private patients have a contract with a particular professional and/or the hospital, and negligent treatment or care may amount to a breach of contract (as well as negligence). Under the Supply of Goods and Services Act 1982 the medical professional or hospital must use 'reasonable care and skill' in treating and caring for patients. In many cases, the distinction between a case in contract and a case in tort will be academic, but sometimes it will be an advantage to rely on both in the alternative (such as when there is a limitation issue).

What compensation can be claimed?

A claimant must prove that the negligence caused the injury complained of. Sometimes, the negligence will have caused the claimant an actual injury. In other circumstances, the claimant will have a reduced chance of recovering or an increased risk of complications in the future. Whatever the nature of the injury, the court must be persuaded that the medical negligence is more likely than not to blame. The amount of damages is worked out in the same way as other personal injury damages; see further under chapter 5, ' How compensation is calculated'.

Hobbies and holidays

Participants in sporting events and other pastimes

Many sports, especially those involving physical contact, carry the inherent risk of injury. A claimant must prove that someone owed him a duty to take care to avoid injuring him. A court will take into consideration all the circumstances of the sport generally. Expert evidence from experienced coaches, umpires, referees or other officials may have to be obtained. Various duties have been considered by the courts and negligence may result from a failure to train participants adequately, or from a failure to maintain equipment properly. Other duties are discussed below.

Highlight

If the player made an error of judgement that no reasonable player would have made, and injured someone as a result, then he will be held to be negligent.

- Where a participant injures another during the course of the activity or match he may be liable for a damages claim. Some allowance is given for things done in the heat of the excitement of a match, and a breach of the rules of the game (such as a foul) does not necessarily amount to negligence. However, if the player made an error of judgement that no reasonable player would have made, and injured someone as a result, then he will be held to be negligent.

- In relation to the supervision and control of the game or match by the referee or umpire, a recent case suggests that the referee or umpire has a duty to control the game so as to avoid 'unnecessary' risk to the claimant participant. What constitutes as 'unnecessary' (or 'necessary') risk in the particular circumstances will have to decided in each case. The umpire or referee must take account of the fact that people under 18 may have less anticipation of the risk of injury to themselves and to others, and alter the way he controls or supervises the game or match.

Spectators

Accidents to spectators may have various causes. Where the condition of the sports ground, arena, buildings, access ways and seating, etc., results in the injury, the claim may be based on the Occupiers' Liability Act or negligence (see 'Accidents on (or in) private property', page 13). Other causes of injury could include poor crowd control or inadequate safety barriers. The claimant must prove that, in the circumstances, the organisers or other people had a duty of care towards him to take care of his safety, and that they breached the duty (negligence).

Accidents abroad

This guide is concerned with claims brought in the English and Welsh courts under English law, which is the proper place to bring a claim where the accident happened in England or Wales and the defendant is based in England or Wales. However, England/Wales may not be the correct place to bring a claim where the accident takes place in another part of the UK (Scotland and Northern Ireland have separate legal systems), or abroad.

European countries

Countries in the European Union and EFTA (Austria, Belgium, Denmark, Finland, France, Germany, Greece, Italy, Luxembourg, The Netherlands, Portugal, Republic of Ireland, Spain, Sweden, the United Kingdom, Iceland, Norway and Switzerland) have subscribed to the Brussels and Lugano Conventions. The Conventions regulate where a personal injury case may be heard.

Tort

The general rule is that a claim in 'tort' (negligence, assault and battery or breach of statutory duty) will be heard in the country in which the defendant is 'domiciled'. A person is domiciled in the country if he has residence that is not just temporary or transient; a company is domiciled in a country where it has its 'seat of business' (usually the place where it is incorporated and registered, or where its central management and control is situated). However, the claim may instead be brought in the country where the 'harm' occurred.

Contract

Where the claim is founded upon a breach of contract (even if it also contains an alternative claim in tort) the claim should be brought in the country where the contract was to be 'performed' (i.e. fulfilled).

Scotland or Northern Ireland

Accidents occurring in Scotland and Northern Ireland are similarly governed by the Civil Jurisdiction and Judgments Act 1982. The basic rule is that a claim based on 'tort' should be brought in the area within the UK where the defendant is 'domiciled' (see above) but may (if different) be brought in the area where the 'harm' took place.

Elsewhere

Where an injury occurs abroad in a non-Convention country (see above), the claimant may be able to bring a claim in the English/Welsh courts if he serves the defendant with the claim form when the defendant is on English/Welsh soil. However, the defendant may be able to persuade the court to halt ('stay') the proceedings if England/Wales is not a convenient forum. Otherwise, the claimant must seek legal advice in the country in which he suffered the injury and, if appropriate, bring a claim there.

Injuries caused by animals

The following section deals with the various 'causes of action' that may arise in relation to animals that cause accidents. More than one cause of action may be applicable; if that is so, the case will be put on alternative bases in the Particulars of Claim.

The Animals Act 1971

Under the Animals Act 1971 a 'keeper' of a dangerous animal is liable for any damage it causes. An animal is classed as dangerous if it belongs to a dangerous species (i.e. a species that is not commonly domesticated in the British Isles and when adult has characteristics that makes it likely to cause severe damage if not restrained). Thus bears, lions and elephants have all been held to be dangerous species. An animal that does not belong to a dangerous species may be classed as 'dangerous' if the keeper knows that his animal has abnormal characteristics (for example, aggressive tendencies) generally or in particular circumstances, and the type of damage likely to be caused by the particular animal is to be severe. Dogs, which are not a 'dangerous species', may nonetheless be 'dangerous' within the meaning of the Act if they have unusual tendencies. In one case, a keeper was found liable when his dog, known to attack people carrying bags, caused damage. Damage caused by an animal that is behaving in a way that is normal or expected may not give rise to a liability.

Claims under the Animal Act 1971 do not have to prove that the keeper was to blame for the animal causing the damage. The essence of the claim is that the keeper of a dangerous animal is liable for damage (including injury) by that animal. A 'keeper' is defined as someone who owns or has the animal in his possession, or where a person under the age of 16 owns or has the animal in his possession the 'head of the household' he belongs to.

Contributory negligence by the claimant is likely to be a significant defence in cases of this type. In other words, the defendant may want to prove that the claimant brought the attack upon himself, for example, by climbing into a lion's cage or taunting a guard dog. The defence that the claimant voluntarily accepted the risk of damage may also feature, for example intervening in a fight between two dogs or trespassing into an enclosure which contains a guard dog. For further discussion of general defences, see chapter 2.

Other personal injury claims involving animals

The Dangerous Dogs Act 1991 – introduced with maximum publicity and often criticised – regulates the keeping of pit-bull terriers, tosas and other proscribed breeds. It creates various

Highlight

Under the Animals Act 1971 a 'keeper' of a dangerous animal is liable for any damage it causes.

criminal offences, but does not directly provide a civil cause of action. The matter is open to consideration by the courts. In any event, most situations will be covered by the Animals Act 1971 or common law 'negligence'. Of course it is open to the victim of an attack by one of the proscribed breeds of dog to report the matter to the police. Where the controller of the dog is convicted of an offence under the Act, the victim may apply for a compensation order or an award by the Criminal Injuries Compensation Board.

A person in charge of an animal may be held to have been negligent if he fails to restrain it suitably and it causes damage or injury to another. Cases may include those arising from attacks by animals, or accidents caused by straying or escaping animals. The court will consider whether in all the circumstances (including the species and usual behaviour of the animal in question, the nature of that particular animal and the foreseeable dangers ahead) the person in charge of the animal has a duty to take care to avoid the danger occurring. The law requires a person to take only 'reasonable' care in the circumstances, not to guard against every eventuality.

Injuries and stress caused to the victims of crime

A person intentionally or 'recklessly' causing an injury to another may have committed a crime. Offences include 'grievous bodily harm', 'actual bodily harm', 'common assault', putting a person in fear of violence, indecent assault and rape. In the civil courts these offences are all classed as 'battery' (and may include 'assault' – see below). Assault and battery are causes of action and will give rise to a claim for damages. Additionally the offence of harassment gives rise to a claim under the Protection from Harassment Act 1997. False imprisonment is an offence that gives rise to a claim under the common law tort of 'false imprisonment' in the civil courts. These causes of action are discussed below. Drivers convicted of 'careless' or 'dangerous' driving will also have been 'negligent' in civil law terms and thereby liable for damages (see 'Road traffic accidents', page 3).

Thus the victim may have a claim in the civil courts for damages as claimant, and also be a prosecution witness against the defendant in the criminal courts. If by the time of the civil trial the defendant has been convicted the evidence of his conviction (a certificate obtained from the convicting court) is evidence that the crime has been committed. In practice, it is unlikely that a convicted defendant will contest a civil action on the basis of liability (although he may contest the amount of damages claimed by the claimant). Note that this rule does not apply to people who have been convicted or acquitted of the various types of assaults or battery in the criminal courts. Such people are exempt from further proceedings for the same incident, either civil or criminal (sections 44 and 45 Offences Against the Person Act 1848). Therefore the only options open to the victims of such crimes are a) to seek a 'compensation order' from the sentencing court upon conviction of the defendant, or b) claim for damages in the civil courts where the CPS have decided not to prosecute or continue to prosecute the defendant. If the defendant is prosecuted and is acquitted the claimant will have no further 'come-back'. The victim of crimes other than the various assaults and battery has therefore two options: a) make a claim for damages in the civil courts and/or b) report the matter to the police and give evidence at trial against the perpetrator.

There are various points to note about each method. Pursuing the matter in the civil courts may be costlier (see page 70, 'How do I fund my claim or defence?') in the long run. Damages in the civil courts tend to be higher than compensation orders, or awards by the Criminal Injuries Compensation Board (although if the defendant is uninsured or has no significant assets he may not have the money to pay the damages awarded anyway). The civil courts have a lower 'standard of proof' than the criminal courts. In the criminal trial, the prosecution must prove 'beyond reasonable doubt' that the offence was committed. To put it another way, the jury or magistrates must be 'satisfied that they are sure' that the defendant did the acts alleged. In the civil courts, on the other hand, the judge has to be satisfied 'on the balance of probabilities' that the defendant did the act complained of. In other words, the judge must be satisfied that the matters complained of 'probably' occurred. The bringing of a civil action for damages is not the same thing as a 'private prosecution' where a private individual rather than the Crown prosecutes a defendant. Private prosecutions, which are within the realm of the criminal law are not within the scope of a guide to personal injury law.

Highlight

In practice, it is unlikely that a convicted defendant will contest a civil action on the basis of liability (although he may contest the amount of damages claimed by the claimant).

Assault and battery

An 'assault', technically, does not involve physical contact. An assault is committed when the defendant, acting deliberately or negligently, causes the claimant to fear that he (the defendant) is about to inflict physical contact on him. Thus it is about the fear of the threat of violence, rather than actual bodily violence. Therefore, shaking a fist at someone may in certain circumstances amount to an 'assault'.

The tort of 'battery' is the deliberate unlawful infliction of force on the person of another. The physical contact need not be violent as such and there does not need to be an intention to cause an injury; a mere touch may constitute a battery. Of course, the courts recognise that a certain amount of physical contact is part of everyday life and not every touch will amount to a cause of action. It is interesting to note that many medical procedures may amount to a battery (for example, internal examinations, or surgery) However, such a battery may not be 'actionable' as the claimant will have consented to the procedure (see further at page 31 'Clinical negligence' for a fuller discussion of assault and battery in medical contexts). Similarly, the punishment of a child by a parent may or may not amount to an unlawful assault and battery depending on whether the defendant parent can establish a defence of 'justification' (see below).

Highlight

The courts recognise that a certain amount of physical contact is part of everyday life and not every touch will amount to a cause of action.

In practical terms, any physical contact that results in an injury will be an actionable battery. In the split second before the attack (or for even longer than that) the claimant might have been aware of the impending battery and therefore suffered an assault as well. Usually the two are termed together 'assault and battery' and where injury has resulted the court is not likely to split hairs over the precise difference.

The defences of 'consent' and 'justification' are available in civil claims for assault and battery. Where the claimant has consented, actually or implied, to the type and degree of physical contact inflicted then the claim for battery will not succeed. If the physical contact exceeds the degree or is of a different type of that consented to, then the claimant will have a claim in battery. Consent that has been obtained through fraud, or some form of coercion is not true consent and is not therefore a defence as such. 'Justification' is where the defendant can prove to the court's satisfaction that the circumstances make the assault and battery 'lawful'. Established circumstances for the layman include self-defence; reasonable force used to prevent a crime or breach of the peace; assisting officers of the law; and the claimant's being in a state of danger to himself or others. Another well-known example of justification is the reasonable chastisement of a child by a parent or other person in authority over the child (in loco parentis). For further discussion of general defences, see chapter 2, 'Defences'.

The deliberate infliction of psychiatric injury

By case law, following the decision of Wilkinson v Downton (1897), a claimant can recover damages for a psychiatric condition brought on by the deliberate actions of the defendant. It was designed to catch those cases where the defendant had deliberately set out to harm the claimant, where no physical assault and battery had occurred. Nowadays, most situations are probably covered by the 'new' statutory tort of harassment – see below.

Harassment

In June 1997, the Protection from Harassment Act came into force. It had been brought in as a result of a perception that there was no effective law against 'stalking', although it is generally thought to apply to non-stalking situations as well. The Act created a new civil 'tort' of harassment (section 3) as well as the criminal offences of harassment and 'putting a person in fear of violence'. It does not define harassment, except to state that it is behaviour that occurs on more than one occasion. In other words harassment is a 'course of conduct'. It is expected that over the next few years the courts will begin to define harassment, although already commentators make it clear that harassment is not necessarily confined to 'stalking-type' behaviour. Nuisance telephone calls, malicious letters, threatening behaviour, intimidation, pestering and other forms of anti-social behaviour directed against one or more people may all amount to harassment.

A successful claimant can recover damages for not only financial loss resulting from the harassment, but also for 'anxiety'. This is unusual in the law of personal injury. Anxiety or distress falling short of psychiatric injury do not normally give rise to a claim for

Highlight

It is expected that over the next few years the courts will begin to define harassment, although already commentators make it clear that harassment is not necessarily confined to 'stalking-type' behaviour.

damages in their own right. In negligence claims, for example, only 'mental injuries' that result in a recognised psychiatric illness give rise to damages. See also 'Compensation for 'pain, suffering and loss of amenity'', page 130, for further discussion on this topic. It remains to be seen how the courts quantify damages for anxiety and other forms of personal injury under the Protection from Harassment Act 1997.

False imprisonment

False imprisonment is a crime as well as a civil wrong. It is the deliberate or reckless restraint of the victim's freedom of movement from a particular place. The restraint may be achieved by physical means or intimidation. The victim need not have been 'taken prisoner' as such. Merely blocking the victim's means of exit or escape will be sufficient. The victim need not realise that he is being restrained. However, lawful restraint (such as lawful arrest) cannot amount to false imprisonment.

Fatal accidents

Where someone dies as a result of an accident, there are two relevant causes of action which arise:

a) On behalf of the deceased for personal injury suffered prior to death (including those sustained in the fatal accident itself) under Section 1 of the Law Reform (Miscellaneous Provisions) Act 1934. This claim is brought by the deceased's executors and any award of damages is paid into the deceased's estate to be distributed according to the will or under the rules of intestacy.

b) On behalf of the deceased's dependants for their own losses arising from the deceased's death, under the Fatal Accidents Act 1976.

A claim may be brought under both Acts for the different types of damage in respect of one fatal accident. No claims can be made, however, where the deceased made a claim relating to the accident that either succeeded, failed or was settled before death occurred. (However, if the deceased was awarded provisional damages before he died, claims under the Acts may be brought. In those circumstances no award will be made for the future loss of earnings which the deceased could have claimed if he had lived.)

Claims on behalf of the deceased (Law Reform (Miscellaneous Provisions) Act 1934)

With the exception of defamation, all the claims or potential claims a person has at the time of death continue after his death. The 'personal representatives' (executors or administrators) step into the deceased's shoes, so to speak, to start or continue any litigation. The law imposes a time limit on when claims may be started and this topic is discussed under 'Is it too late to sue?' on page 63 and 'Fatal accidents' on page 67.

This means that where an accident immediately or ultimately caused the death of the victim, the executors or personal representative become the claimants in any case. The normal rules apply; they must bring evidence to prove that the injuries resulted from the defendant's wrongdoing (negligence, breach of statutory duty, breach of contract, nuisance, etc.). There are certain types of damage that cannot be recovered in such an action, many of which will be self-evident:

a) damages for bereavement;

b) any loss of income after the date of death;

c) exemplary damages;

d) except for the funerary expenses, losses to his estate as a result of the death, which are really losses that will be suffered by the dependants or legatees rather than the deceased himself.

Other types of damage may be recovered to the extent that the deceased suffered – see further at page 130, 'Compensation for 'pain, suffering and loss of amenity''; page 134, 'Compensation for financial loss and expenses up to the date of trial or settlement' and page 135, 'Compensation for future losses and expenses'.

Awards in these sort of proceedings may be small, as they will not include any sum for future losses, such as future loss of earnings, which often make up the greater proportion of awards. The court will have to assess exactly what pain, suffering and loss of amenity the deceased endured between the accident and death.

Highlight

Where an accident immediately or ultimately caused the death of the victim, the executors or personal representative become the claimants in any case.

Therefore, in cases where the deceased died instantly, awards for pain, suffering and loss of amenity may be inappropriate. Conversely, in cases where the deceased lived some considerable time before death the damages are likely to be high. The court will take into account that for the periods the deceased was unconscious, he was unlikely to have had pain or other suffering, and will reduce the award accordingly. Some 'special damages' may be appropriate, such as a damaged vehicle or increased medical expenses; see page 134, 'Compensation for financial loss and expenses up to the date of trial or settlement.'

Claims on behalf the deceased's dependants (under the Fatal Accidents Act 1976)

A claim may be brought for the benefit of the deceased's dependants against the person whose wrongful act caused the death of the deceased. The 'wrongful act' may be negligence, breach of statutory duty or other causes of action in the normal way and reference should be made to earlier parts of this chapter. The personal representatives (executors under the will or the administrators under the intestacy provisions) are named as claimants, except where they have failed to bring the claim within six months of the death, when the dependant(s) themselves bring the claim.

Who may be awarded damages?

Dependants are defined in the Act as:

a)   the deceased's spouse or former spouse;

b)   any person living with the deceased as the husband or wife of the deceased at the date of death and for at least two years before the date of death;

c)   any parent or other ascendant of the deceased's or any person whom the deceased treated as a parent;

d)   any child or other descendant of the deceased;

e)   any child who, although not the deceased's own child, was treated by the deceased as a child of the family (during the time the deceased was married, at least);

f)   any child of the deceased's brother, sister, aunt or uncle or any child of the deceased's spouse's brother, sister, aunt or uncle.

The amount of damages

The award will reflect the financial losses of the dependants, rather than any injury, loss or damage suffered by the deceased. The court will only award the following:

a)   £7,500 damages for 'bereavement' – only to the spouse of the deceased, or where the deceased was under the age of 18 and never married, to his parents (if he was legitimate) or to his mother only (where he was illegitimate);

b)   the amount the deceased would have given to his dependant;

c)   any extra expenses the dependant has incurred as a result of the deceased's death;

d)   any particular losses the dependant has suffered as a result of the deceased's death.

Although it may not be possible to be exact about the figures, the court will strive to make its estimation of the losses suffered by the dependants as a result of the accident and death. Various methods are used by the courts to establish what each dependant should be awarded. Where the deceased was working, it may be a matter of simply working out what percentage of his earnings would be available for the dependants.

Once the value of the dependency is ascertained the court will take into account:

a)   any 'contributory negligence' on the part of the deceased (see page 51, 'Defences');

b)   interest;

c)   any benefits or savings made as a result of the accident by the deceased, including contractual sick pay, social security benefits, some pension payments, some redundancy payouts, savings on living expenses caused by a stay in hospital or similar provider; see further at page 135, 'DSS benefits and the Compensation Recovery Unit 'clawback" and page 139, 'Insurance payouts and other deductions';

d) the proportion each dependant should receive of the calculated amount;

e) any award of damages for bereavement (currently set at £7,500).

Defences

2

If the 'pre-action protocol' has been followed, the defendant will have a fairly good idea of the claimant's case from an early stage (see further under 'The first step in litigation: 'pre-action protocols'' on page 83). In order to comply with his own obligation under the protocol, the defendant is required to consider his own position when he receives notification of a potential claim. The defendant may consider that the claimant has the facts wrong, or there may be justification for his actions, or that there is a technical defence available to him. These factors may enable the defendant to deny that he is liable to the claimant. Furthermore, the claimant may have put in a claim for items or amounts that the law does not entitle him to recover. He may be able to challenge the 'quantum' or amount of the claim, even if he admits liability.

Whatever defence is relied upon, it is important to remember that the Defence form must be verified by a 'statement of truth'; the defendant must confirm that the facts contained in the defence document are true. A defendant who has signed the statement not believing the truth of the facts in the defence is 'in contempt of court'. The court may bring proceedings against him for the contempt. Contempt of court is punishable by up to two years in prison and/or a fine.

The Defence form is a document that the defendant uses to tell the court and the claimant of his defence. It should carefully set out his response to each of the allegations made by the claimant. Every statement made by the claimant in the Particulars of Claim must either be:

a) 'admitted' – in which case the issue is no longer 'live' and the court accepts the fact without hearing any evidence from either party;

b) 'not admitted' – where the defendant has no knowledge or evidence of whether the allegation is true or not, and therefore simply requires the claimant to call evidence to prove the fact; or

c) 'denied' – where the defendant disagrees with the fact or entitlement alleged and puts forward his own version; the court will hear evidence (or legal argument if appropriate) from both sides and make findings as to which version it prefers.

Example

The Particulars of Claim reads:

1. *The parties were involved in a road traffic accident at about 6.30 am on the 20th August 2001 at the 'Waterboys Roundabout' on the A4.*

2. *The claimant was the owner and driver of a red Peugeot 106 registration XXXXX. The defendant was the driver of a green Mazda registration number YYYYYY.*

3. *The collision occurred between the two vehicles described above when the defendant drove his car into the claimant's. The said collision was caused by the negligence of the defendant.*

   PARTICULARS OF NEGLIGENCE...........

4. *As a result of the matters set out above the claimant suffered loss and damage and was injured*

   PARTICULARS OF LOSS...........

   PARTICULARS OF INJURY.........

The defendant, on reading the Particulars of Claim, agrees that a collision took place between him and the claimant at the date, time and location alleged. These facts will be agreed. However, he believes that although his car physically drove into the claimant's, this was not due to any negligent driving on his part, but rather to the claimant's own negligent driving. As he was not to blame for the accident, neither is he to blame for any loss and injury alleged by the claimant. These issues therefore the defendant should deny. Finally, he has no evidence of his own as to the damage and loss and injury suffered by the claimant and therefore should challenge him to prove his losses and the entitlement to them by 'not admitting' them.

It is always helpful to go through the Particulars of Claim and identify each allegation and how it is going to be answered.

ADMIT	NOT ADMIT	DENY	ASSERT
I am the person named as defendant	The loss the claimant claims	That I was negligent	It was his negligent driving that caused the accident
I was involved in an accident with the claimant the location is correct the date and time are correct	The injury		

The Defence may therefore read like this:

1. Paragraphs 1 and 2 of the Particulars of Claim are admitted.

2. The defendant admits that the collision occurred when he drove his car into the claimant's vehicle; however, the defendant denies driving negligently as alleged in Paragraph 3 of the Particulars of Claim or at all.

3. The collision was caused by the negligent driving of the claimant in that he:

   PARTICULARS OF NEGLIGENCE
   [*set out each allegation of the claimant's negligence here*]

   Alternatively, the claimant's negligent driving as set out above contributed to the accident.

4. The defendant denies causing the alleged loss, damage and injury. Moreover, the defendant does not admit the type and amount of loss, damage and injury as alleged in Paragraph 4 of the Particulars of Claim.

Sample paragraphs to be included in the Defence form are set out in Appendix 2. Sample paragraphs for use when making a Counterclaim (also known as a 'Part 20 claim') can be found in Appendix 2, page 166. Further information about dealing with Particulars of Claim is found under 'Defendant: how to deal with the Response Pack' on page 93.

Denying liability

Denying legal entitlement

The claimant must satisfy the court that the defendant is legally liable to compensate him for each item of injury and loss. His claim is founded upon a 'cause of action' (for example, negligence, breach of statutory duty, battery, harassment, etc.). A close analysis of the Particulars of Claim may reveal that a crucial element in the cause of action is not present. For example, a particular Act of Parliament or set of regulations on which the claimant is seeking to rely does not apply to the defendant (or to the claimant or to the situation generally, as the case may be). Similarly, the claimant might not have alleged a fact crucial to the cause of action. There is no need to argue complex points of law in the defence, but it should clearly allege that the claim fails to amount to negligence/battery/breach of statutory regulation, etc. See sample paragraphs 1 and 5 in Appendix 2, page 165.

Highlight

A close analysis of the Particulars of Claim may reveal that a crucial element in the cause of action is not present.

Challenging the facts

Many cases will come down to a straightforward fight on the facts. The essence of this type of defence is that the defendant (a) challenges the claimant's evidence and (b) brings his own evidence in order to persuade the court that the claimant has not proved negligence, battery, breach of statutory duty, etc. See sample paragraphs 2-5 and 7-9 set out in Appendix 2, pages 165-6.

Denying causation

The claimant must prove that the defendant's behaviour or omission caused his loss and injury. Where there is no evidence to prove this, or the claimant's evidence has been successfully discredited by the defendant at trial, a crucial element of his cause of action, namely 'causation', has not been proved. He should state clearly in the Defence that he denies that any behaviour on his part (whether admitted or not) caused the claimant's loss and injury.

Challenging the claimant's evidence of causation may be a matter of common sense. In some situations, however, the judge may need the assistance of specialist help (perhaps, for example, whether a particular chemical caused a disease; whether a mechanical failure caused a crash; whether a surgical treatment caused an injury; or whether a claimant's pre-existing medical condition was made worse by an injury). It may therefore be necessary to call expert evidence to prove or challenge 'causation', as well as to give opinion on other matters. Expert evidence is dealt with under 'Expert evidence', on page 108.

Injury caused by something beyond his control

Where the defendant has committed a wrongful act towards the claimant, but another factor that is beyond the defendant's control then contributes to the claimant's injury loss or damage, the court must decide if the defendant is responsible to the claimant. This principle was known as *novus actus interveniens*; in other words, the 'intervening act' has broken the series of events between the defendant's wrong and the claimant's loss injury and damage.

The court will look carefully at the chain of events leading up to the injury to see if the factor (whether an act of nature, the act of a third party, or the act of the claimant) introduced a new, possibly unforeseen, element into what has happened.

Contributory negligence ━━━━━

The defendant may allege that the claimant's actions or omissions were the only cause of the loss or injury complained of, rather than anything defendant has done or failed to do. In that case, he is asserting that the claimant has failed to make out the cause of action (see above). However, where the defendant believes that the claimant by his action or inaction was partly to blame for the loss and injury suffered, he can rely on section 1 of the Law Reform (Contributory Negligence) Act 1945. If the court finds that the accident is partly the fault of the claimant, the claimant's damages will be reduced proportionately to the extent to which he was to blame. Thus the claimant who is found to have been 50 per cent to blame for the accident or injury will have his damages reduced by 50 per cent. An example of this 'defence' can be found at paragraph 11 in Appendix 2, page 166.

A claimant who contributed to his own injury by reacting in the 'agony of the moment' will not be held to be contributorily negligent.

Legal defences ——————————

Claimant knows about and accepts the risk of the defendant's behaviour

If successful, this defence has the effect of ruling that even though the defendant's actions caused the injury and loss, the claimant is to blame for his own injury. The defendant must prove that the claimant, by his words or actions at the time of the accident, has voluntarily waived his right to claim against the defendant for the risk posed by the defendant's behaviour. The defence will not succeed where the claimant merely knew about the risk. It is unlikely to apply in accident at work claims.

Limitation

The Limitation Act 1980 places a time limit on the period in which the claimant may bring a claim against the defendant; once the relevant time limit has expired, the defendant may assert that the claim is 'statute barred'. Even the strongest claim cannot proceed once a successful limitation defence has been proved. However, the defendant must be careful to raise the issue himself. The claimant will not mention it. The only way for the court to hear argument that the claim is statute-barred by the Limitation Act (or other provision) is for the defendant to include the appropriate paragraph in the Defence form. Of, course he need not rely on it if he does not want to and he may also formally waive the right to rely on the Act.

The Act sets out various 'limitation periods'. Most claims based on personal injuries will have a limitation period of three years, which can be extended in certain circumstances. A six-year rule

Highlight

A claimant who contributed to his own injury by reacting in the 'agony of the moment' will not be held to be contributorily negligent.

applies to some causes of action. There are special rules dealing with child claimants and 'patients' under the Mental Health Act. To find out what limitation period applies to the claim and for a discussion of how to calculate the period see under 'Is it too late to sue?' on page 63. A sample limitation defence is shown in Appendix 2, at paragraph 10, on page 166.

The claimant was himself acting wrongfully

The fact that the claimant was acting wrongfully or even illegally is not usually relevant to a claim for personal injury and will not amount to a defence. Only in certain exceptional cases will the court decide that a claimant was acting so wrongfully or illegally at the time the defendant was negligent or in breach of statutory duty, etc. that he should not benefit from legal process. The case law in this area is somewhat complex and possibly contradictory, and a discussion of this area (known by its Latin 'tag' as *ex turpi causa non oritur actio*) is outside the scope of this guide.

Reasonableness

There are two ways in which the defendant's reasonableness is a defence:

1. In certain situations, Acts of Parliament or regulations provide that if the defendant can prove he was in fact acting reasonably in the circumstances he will not be liable. An example of this is the Protection against Harassment Act 1997. This defence may therefore amount to a justification of the defendant's otherwise wrongful actions.

2. Other legislation and rules of law provide that the defendant only has to act reasonably or take reasonable steps in the circumstances to ensure the claimant's safety, etc. Thus the defendant, in proving he has taken those reasonable steps or acted reasonably, disproves the claimant's claim that he has breached a duty towards him. An example of where this might be an issue is the (defendant) driver's duty to take reasonable care for the safety of other road users.

Either way, if the defendant is successful, the claimant will not be able to succeed on his claim. Defendants should look carefully at the legislation that the claimant is relying upon to see if this defence is available. A sample paragraph for inclusion in the Defence is shown at paragraph 6, on page 165, Appendix 2.

Challenging the amount of damages claimed

Types of damage may not be recoverable

It is worth checking that each item of damage claimed is something that the court will order compensation for. A discussion about what types of loss, injury and damage the claimant can recover damages for is found under 'How compensation is calculated' on page 129. If an item is not recoverable, the defendant should state in the defence that the entitlement to it (or the type of loss or damage) is disputed.

Failure to mitigate loss

The claimant has a general duty to 'mitigate his loss'. This means that he must take reasonable steps to minimise his expenses and losses (including future losses) caused by the defendant's action. Everything will depend on the circumstances of the case and the options open to the claimant, as his loss and expenses become clear after the incident. For example, the court may decide that it would have been reasonable for the claimant to have undertaken recommended medical treatment, or retrained so as to obtain future employment, or to have used a contractor who provided the lowest estimate. If the claimant has incurred extra expense or increased his damage or injury by not taking these reasonable steps, that extra expense or increased expense will not be awarded in damages. Accordingly, where this defence succeeds it takes the form of (a) a reduction of the amount claimed for an item of loss or injury, or (b) no award of damages with respect to a particular item of loss or injury.

Highlight

It is worth checking that each item of damage claimed is something that the court will order compensation for

3

Evidence

What is evidence?

The claimant must prove his claim against the defendant – this means that he must establish the facts that give rise to the defendant's liability to pay him damages (known as proving 'liability'). He must also bring evidence as to the amount of his loss, injury or damage (known as proving 'quantum'). He does this by 'adducing evidence'; in other words, formally submitting evidence to the judge. During the trial, the judge will be taken through all the different types of evidence. That evidence will be 'tested' by the defendant in cross-examination. The defendant will also point out weaknesses and gaps in the claimant's evidence. In cases where the defendant is putting forward an alternative version of events or a different explanation of what happened, the defendant will adduce his own evidence. The claimant then has the opportunity to test the defendant's evidence.

Clearly, then, evidence is crucial to a case because it is upon tested evidence that the judge makes his decisions. Both parties must think very carefully about what evidence they need to obtain. There must be evidence to support every element of the claim (or defence).

Types of evidence

Oral evidence

Oral evidence is evidence given by witnesses in court. However, claimants and defendants are also required to obtain written witness statements from all the witnesses they intend to call. (See page 104, 'Witness statements'). As the written witness statement is available at the trial, the witness usually will adopt the contents of the witness statement and then move straight on to cross-examination (see 'The trial', page 114.)

The responsibility for paying the expenses of a witness to come to court and a certain amount for lost earnings, or the professional fee of an expert witness, falls on the party calling that witness. However, these costs may be repaid by the other party if the court orders him to (see page 119, 'Costs').

Witnesses of fact

Witnesses of fact are called by a party to tell the court what they have seen or heard. The parties themselves (the claimant and defendant) of course may give their own evidence. There may be other people who saw something relating to the accident or incident. Others might be able to give evidence of background circumstances if relevant. If their evidence (as shown in a witness statement before 'disclosure' – see below) is unfavourable, one does not have to use it at trial, or even disclose it. However, it may be that the other party might call them, and they are free to do so.

Expert witnesses

A party should call an expert witness if evidence of a technical subject is necessary. Almost all personal injury claims will involve at least the evidence of a medical specialist, who is able to tell the court what injuries were suffered, whether the incident was likely to have 'caused' the injuries, indicate the likely prognosis and other such details.

Other types of claim will require different sorts of specialist. For example, a mechanical engineer will be able to explain how a defect in a vehicle (which he has examined) caused an accident;

Highlight

Witnesses of fact are called by a party to tell the court what they have seen or heard. The parties themselves (the claimant and defendant) of course may give their own evidence an employment specialist will be able (having interviewed the claimant and with local knowledge of the labour market) to give evidence of the claimant's chances of future employment, etc. For further information about instructing an expert witness see under 'Expert evidence' on page 108.

Documentary or paper evidence

There are many different types of document that may be relevant to the case which can be included in the evidence 'adduced' by a party. Receipts, invoices, estimates, employee records, hospital and other medical records, accident books, police reports, etc. may all have relevance to the case.

Highlight

It is for the parties to decide what disclosed material to 'adduce' as evidence at trial.

Documents that are relevant must be 'disclosed' to the other party, although there is no need to disclose 'without prejudice' correspondence or communications (see Glossary). For further discussion on 'disclosure' of documentary evidence, see under 'Directions for trial'. It is for the parties to decide what disclosed material to 'adduce' as evidence at trial. Once documentary evidence is 'disclosed' either or both parties may want to rely on it as evidence. Thus if one party disclosed a document but does not want to rely on it as evidence, it is perfectly proper for the other party to cross-examine him about it, or otherwise bring it to the judge's attention and rely on it.

Physical evidence (and recorded physical evidence)

There are many occasions where a case can be better presented by the production of physical evidence. This may take the form of photographic or video evidence, or it may entail a physical object being brought to court and 'exhibited' by a witness (formally announced as part of that witness's evidence). Photographs of the site of an accident are usually very useful, for example, in road traffic accidents or accidents at work or relating to the state of property. Where equipment has been defective or inadequate, the object itself may be exhibited, or photographs if more appropriate. On rare occasions, the judge may consider (or be persuaded) that a 'site' view is necessary; this involves all the parties and their lawyers meeting with the judge at the site so that the judge has the opportunity of 'seeing it for himself'.

Collecting evidence

The responsibility for collecting (and disclosing) the evidence falls to the party who intends to rely on it. The parties will be given a time limit to put the evidence they have collected into a suitable form for the trial; see under 'Directions for trial'. Of course much of the evidence will have been gathered and shown to the other side long before that stage, as each party must comply with the pre-action protocol (see under 'The first step in litigation: 'pre-action protocols', page 83).

Obtaining evidence from witnesses of fact (eyewitnesses)

The first stage is to find the names and addresses of those who might be able to help you. The potential witnesses may be people known to you, they may be passers-by who offer to help, or they may have given their details to the police. Indeed, if the police attended the scene, you should write to the relevant police station asking for the official police report (a small fee will be charged). The second stage is to find out whether the witnesses (a) have any useful evidence to give and (b) are willing to give evidence. If willing, the witness should be asked to write down what they saw or heard. The third stage is for the party to put the evidence in the form it needs to be for the court. The court will direct the parties to exchange witness statements (see page 104, 'Witness statements').

It may be that the witness has already made his statement in the appropriate form, complying with the standard formal format (described on pages 104 and 106). If not, it may be sensible to type (or write out legibly) the statement adding the necessary formalities, such as the sentence '*I [name] of [address] will say as follows....*' or the 'statement of truth' (see pages 104 and 106). Leave a space blank for the witness to sign and date the statement and send it back to him. A discussion of what a witness statement should contain and an example is shown under 'Witness statements'. It should be written in the witness's own words and contain all the evidence he will give. If the witness is exhibiting any documents, photographs, videos or other evidence, remember to identify the exhibit; an example is shown under 'Witness statements'. Make it clear to the witness that if he has any changes

Highlight

If the police attended the scene, you should write to the relevant police station asking for the official police report (a small fee will be charged).

to make to the statement, he should do so and initial the amendments (as one might correct a cheque, for example).

Once you have the returned, signed and dated the statement, you are ready to disclose it to the other side. If, after considering your case, you do not wish to call a particular witness, you are not obliged to disclose the witness statement. If, after disclosing the witness statement to the other side and to the court, you decide not to call that witness, then you do not have to do so (although the other side might want to call the witness anyway, and may obtain a witness summons to compel the witness to appear at trial). Remember to keep copies of witness statements for yourself and for the witness to refer to in the witness box. Finally, do not forget to make your own witness statement, and to include exhibits of all relevant documentation (such as receipts, estimates, and invoices).

Reluctant witnesses

Highlight

If a witness is reluctant to attend court to give oral evidence or to produce documents, the court can order him to attend.

If a witness is reluctant to attend court to give oral evidence or to produce documents, the court can order him to attend. Such an order is called a 'witness summons' (formerly known colloquially as a 'subpoena'). The party wanting to call the witness must ask the court to issue the summons. If there is less than seven days to go before the trial, or the witness is to attend at court on a date other than the formal trial, a judge at the court must give permission for a witness summons to be issued. If permission is needed, an application under Part 23 Civil Proceedings Rules 1998 should be made; see under 'Applications in the period before trial', page 109.

If the witness fails to comply with the summons issued by the High Court, he is in 'contempt of court' (punishable by a fine or up to two years' imprisonment). Disobedience of a witness summons in the county court is punishable by a fine of up to £1,000. The disobedient witness may also be ordered to pay any legal costs which have arisen and have been wasted as a result of his non-compliance.

Obtaining expert evidence

A general discussion of expert evidence is found under 'Expert evidence' on page 108. No expert will be allowed to give evidence for a party unless the court has given permission (even if he has

Specimen letter to a medical expert

Dear [*name of expert*]

I am seeking compensation from [*name*] for injuries I received in an accident which occurred on [*date*]/We are [potential] parties to litigation arising from an accident which occurred on [*date*].

I should be grateful if you could arrange to examine me and produce a full and detailed report. The report should deal with the following:

- any relevant pre-accident medical history
- the injuries received in the above accident
- the treatment I have received
- any recommended future treatment
- my present condition
- causation
- progress of symptoms and prognosis
- the present and future impact of the injuries on my daily living/ability to work

I (We) confirm that I (we) will be (jointly) responsible for your reasonable fees for producing the report.

I (We) enclose copies of my medical records from [*GP's name*] and [*hospital*]/I am ([*name*] is) in the process of obtaining my (his/her) medical records and will send them to you as soon as I have ([he/she] has) received them/Please request my ([*name*]'s) medical records from [*GP's name*] and [*hospital*] and send me (us) a copy of any invoice for this that is sent to you.

Please could you write/telephone me when you receive this letter and confirm the date you will produce your report/The court has ordered me to submit your report by [*date*]; please let me know by return if you will be able to comply with this timescale.

Yours sincerely
A Claimant

already been instructed and/or produced a report). This the judge will consider at the 'directions' stage of preparation for trial. However, by then the parties will already have considered what expert(s) they need, and may already have agreed jointly to instruct experts under the 'pre-action protocols' (see page 83, 'The first step in litigation: 'pre-action protocols''). Note that the expert must be independent (i.e. not be personally or professionally involved in the matter or with either of the parties). The expert must also have the right expertise and experience to help the court in understanding and deciding the technical aspects of the case. Close examination of the prospective expert witness's CV will be necessary. Additionally, experts with 'forensic' experience (i.e. ones who have given evidence in court before) are preferable, as they will be familiar with the way in which courts analyse matters such as causation and prognosis.

Highlight

If the expert is to be instructed jointly, then that must be made clear in the letter, and both parties must agree to the terms of the letter.

An expert must be formally 'instructed' to produce a report. The letter of instruction must be neutral (see example on opposite page). If the expert is to be instructed jointly, then that must be made clear in the letter, and both parties must agree to the terms of the letter.

Collecting documentary evidence

A list of the types of document that are likely to be relevant to certain types of case can be found at Appendix 3. The party who has these documents in his possession should send copies to the other side at the earliest opportunity (such as when the defendant sends his letter rejecting liability at step 3 of the pre-action protocol; see 'The first step in litigation: 'pre-action protocols''). A specimen form for requesting hospital medical records together with the Law Society's note can be found at Appendix 4.

Claiming in the civil courts

4

Is it too late to sue? ▅▅▅▅▅▅

Parliament has decided that the claimant only has a certain amount of time to 'issue' his claim at court (the Limitation Act 1980). Any claim issued after the relevant time is 'statute-barred' and may fail, even if the merits are very strong. The Act lays down various limitation periods for different causes of action. Generally one rule applies to personal injury claims; however, there are separate time limits for claims arising from fatal accidents, assault (battery), wrongful imprisonment, the intentional causing of harm, and defective products. These are considered separately below.

When calculating the date, it is important to realise that the limitation period is calculated *beginning with the day after* the relevant day (usually the day on which the personal injury was sustained). The period will end on the *last day* of the limitation period.

Highlight

A defendant who notices that the relevant time limit has expired can rely on the Limitation Act in court – this is known as raising a 'defence of limitation'.

A defendant who notices that the relevant time limit has expired can rely on the Limitation Act in court – this is known as raising a 'defence of limitation'. The defence is a legal one, and if proved will always succeed, even if the claim is a strong one. It is essential, therefore, for both the claimant and defendant to work out the relevant time limits. However, if the defendant expressly agrees not to rely on a defence of limitation, or accepts liability, or otherwise indicates that the only disagreement relates to the amount of damages, he will be taken to have waived the defence and will not be allowed by the court to rely on it.

Personal injuries arising from negligence, breach of contract or nuisance

'One-off' accidents

Most personal injuries are caused by 'accidents'. A single mishap causes the initial injury *at the time of the accident*. Where this is the case, the claimant has three years from the date of the accident to 'issue' a claim at court (section 11(4)(a) Limitation Act 1980). Such accidents may arise in all sorts of situations: at work, on the roads, in public places or on someone else's land. Note, however, for accidents causing injury to passengers travelling by air and sea, the limitation period is two years; such situations are governed by the Carriage by Air Act 1961, the Maritime Conventions Act 1911 and the Merchant Shipping Act 1995.

Where the personal injury does not arise immediately

In some situations an injury develops some time after a negligent act, breach of contract or act of nuisance. The first the claimant knows about it is when symptoms develop, sometimes years after the event. The law allows him time to discover that (a) the injury is 'significant' enough to make a claim for, (b) to investigate whether the injury is attributable to the actions or omissions of the potential defendant and (c) to discover the identity of the person who is to blame for the injuries and anyone else who is to be a defendant, (see 'Whom to sue?' on page 73). Once the answers to these questions are known, the clock starts running. A claim must be issued within three years of finding out the answers to these questions; this is referred to in the Act as the date of 'knowledge'. The claimant is expected to seek the appropriate expert advice in investigating his claim (expert advice does not include legal advice in this instance) at a reasonable time.

Highlight

For accidents causing injury to passengers travelling by air and sea, the limitation period is two years

Example

Mrs Brown is told by a consultant on the 5th December 2000 that the pains she is suffering are caused by a medical instrument negligently left inside her after an operation four years ago. She knows that her operation was performed by Professor McKay at Anytown District Hospital. Mrs Brown has

three years from the 5th December 2000 to issue a claim against Professor McKay and the Anytown Hospital Trust.

Example

Bhupinder Talal is told by her specialist on the 14th July 2000 that she has developed a rare eye condition. On the 8th August 2000, she is reminded by a friend of an incident of chemical contamination of the local water supply by a water company, that occurred five years before. She consults an expert on water contamination and on the 20th December receives his report that confirms that there is a high likelihood that the contamination caused her particular condition. Miss Talal had three years from the 20th December 2000 to issue a claim against the water company.

When considering a claim, the court may make a decision that the claimant should reasonably have known the relevant facts at a certain date. This may result in the three-year time limit running earlier than the claimant expected. For example, a claimant may have ignored obvious symptoms until after the date on which it would have been reasonable to obtain expert advice. Alternatively, he might not have bothered to find out the identity of a defendant when he should have done. The court will deem the time to start running at an appropriate date; if the claimant issued the claim later than three years from that date, then the claim will fail. However, it may be possible to apply to the court to extend the limitation period.

Where the claimant dies

If the proposed claimant dies (but the case is *not* suitable for a fatal accident claim; see 'Fatal accidents' on page 41) his executors may wish to make a claim for the benefit of the deceased's estate (the money available to be paid out to beneficiaries, etc.), if the deceased had not already begun an action (for a separate prior personal injury). The time limit which applies to the executors or 'personal representatives' is three years from the date of (a) the deceased's death or (b) the executor's or personal representative's 'knowledge' (or if there is more than one of them, the earliest date of the 'knowledge' any of them had), whichever is the later. For a discussion as to what is meant by 'knowledge' see 'Where the personal injury does not arise immediately', above.

Where injuries are caused by repeated acts

Where an injury or disease is caused by repeated wrongful acts, such as an industrial disease caused by repeated exposure to dangerous chemicals, it may be that the claimant can recover damages sustained in the three years immediately prior to the issue of his claim. The defendant must show how much of the damage is attributable to the last three years and if he cannot, he may be held liable for all the damage.

Example

Brian has worked in a very noisy factory since 1990. In 1994, he noticed that he was having hearing problems and on the 1st October 1995 his doctor confirms that the noise in the factory has caused his problems. It seems that the condition will get steadily worse if he continues to work at the factory. Brian does continue in his job and there is no change to the sound levels he is exposed to. On the 1st May 1999, Brian issues a claim for damages against his employer in his local county court. Because the cause of action is 'continuing', in other words the employer is committing a fresh breach of duty every day that Brian goes into work, only the last three years' worth of damage will be considered by the court. Thus, he will probably be able to claim for damages arising on or after the 1st May 1996.

Extending the limitation period

A claimant wishing to issue a claim after the relevant three years may apply to the court to 'disapply' the limitation period. The court will only disapply the limitation period rule if it thinks that the balance of fairness requires it. In other words, it must weigh up the unfairness ('prejudice') to the claimant if, because of the expiry of the limitation period, he would not be able to bring his claim, and the unfairness to the defendant in having a personal

Highlight

The court will only disapply the limitation period rule if it thinks that the balance of fairness requires it.

injury action brought against him after the three years allowed by the law.

An application usually arises once the defendant has 'raised a defence of limitation' in his Defence (see 'Limitation' on page 52). The claimant should apply to the court using a 'Part 23 Application Notice'. The procedure and a sample court form are set out under 'Applications in the period before trial' on page 109. The court, when considering whether to allow the claimant's application, will consider all the circumstances leading up to the decision to issue a claim, including the length and reasons for delay by the claimant, whether or not the quality of the evidence will be affected by the delay, the conduct of the defendant in responding to requests for information, the steps taken by the claimant to obtain legal or expert advice relating to the claim.

Fatal accidents

The Limitation Act 1980 lays down that an action under the Fatal Accidents Act 1976 should be brought within three years of whichever is later, the date of death or the date of the 'knowledge' of the person for whose benefit the action is brought (or dates of knowledge if there is more than one of them). For details of who can begin an action arising from a fatal accident please see 'Fatal Accidents' on page 41. What is meant by the date of 'knowledge' is discussed above under 'Where the injury does not arise immediately'. Note that an application to disapply the time limit may be made. The law and procedure is described above. Note also that in certain circumstances other legislation might apply and different periods may have been set.

Harassment claims

The Protection from Harassment Act 1997 came into force on the 16th July 1997, and thus any act of harassment *on or after* that date may be the subject of a claim (but not acts before that date). The claimant has six years from the day he suffered, or began suffering, the effects of the harassment (anxiety, financial or other loss) to issue the claim.

Assault (battery) and intentional causation of harm

In this situation, the claimant has six years from the date of the act complained of to bring a claim for damages.

Defective products

Where a claim is made under Part 1 of the Consumer Protection Act 1987 (see under 'Defective products' on page 25) for personal injury, the limitation period is usually three years from the date of whichever is later:

- the date the damage or injury was sustained or

- the date of 'knowledge' of the claimant.

Where the proposed claimant dies before issuing his claim relating to the defective product (and there being no grounds to bring a Fatal Accidents Act claim), the deceased's executors or personal representative may wish to bring a claim on behalf of his estate (See 'Can I bring a claim?' on page 80). The executor has three years from (a) the date of the deceased's death or (b) the date of the personal representative's 'knowledge', whichever is the later, to bring the claim.

Do I need a solicitor?

The short answer to the question 'Do I need a solicitor?' is 'No'. Generally, every person has the right to conduct their own case in court. Alternatively, parties may instruct a solicitor to represent them at any stage. If higher court advocacy is involved, a barrister may be instructed by the solicitor on your behalf to conduct hearings and the trial. Trade unions and other interest groups often have legal departments which conduct litigation on behalf of their members. Some of these may be able to instruct 'counsel' (a barrister) directly. However, recent changes to the civil court rules (known as the 'Woolf reforms') have recognised that 'litigants-in-person' are appearing more frequently in the courts. The reforms aim to modernise the rules that govern procedure. Plainer English has been used, for instance, and the one set of rules applies to both county courts and the High Court. Court users will find that the court forms are now accompanied by helpful notes and leaflets are available from court offices to explain some of the more common

Highlight

The short answer to the question 'Do I need a solicitor?' is 'No'.

questions arising from members of the public. Finally, judges are usually alive to the needs of the litigants-in-person.

The question of whether you would be disadvantaged by not having a solicitor is more difficult to answer. The advantage of having a lawyer conduct a case is that the day-to-day management of the case and preparation for trial is out of your hands. A lawyer will be able to spot, and hopefully deal with, the technical problems that often arise, before and during the trial. Furthermore, a lawyer will be used to presenting a case to the court, not only making 'submissions' on the law, but also examining and cross-examining witnesses.

The question will probably come down to three issues: the personality and circumstances of the litigant, the complexity of the case and the financial position of the litigant. Below are some issues that should be taken into account when making the decision on whether or not to instruct a solicitor.

The need to be articulate

Conducting a court case will involve a person in filling in forms, putting a case or witness statement in writing which will be very closely scrutinised by opponent and judge, giving evidence by speaking aloud in court, being cross-examined and cross-examining the other party's witnesses and taking decisions generally about the case. The person who is articulate about his case will be in a stronger position than the one who is not.

The emotional pressures of litigation

The other factor that should not be underestimated is the emotional cost of litigation. A person who is involved in a court case will usually feel aggrieved, either because he has suffered an injury or because he feels wrongly accused. Add to this the stress of having to deal with the bureaucratic side of litigation (with its attendant paperwork, costs and deadlines), and the pressures of simply being in court (finding the courthouse and court room, waiting for the inevitable delays, attending hearings, etc.). The stress of being involved in a court case as a party or witness is great enough; without the support of a lawyer it may be all the greater.

How do I fund my claim or defence?

There are three different types of cost that arise out of a court case:

    (a) court fees;

    (b) costs of legal representation;

    (c) damages.

Court fees and legal representation costs are known as 'costs'. An award of damages is considered separately below. Inevitably both sides will run up such costs, even if a case never gets as far as trial. At the end of the case, the court will make a decision as to whom, if anyone, must pay such costs. The court has absolute discretion (except in the case of Small Claims Track costs which are subject to slightly different rules – see below) and will take into account various matters, including who has 'won' and the behaviour of the parties during the run-up to trial. Costs must also be considered when a settlement is being negotiated, and an agreement to pay some, if not all, costs will often be included in the deal. The court may also decide that nobody should pay anyone else's costs, but that each party should bear his own.

The question of costs must, however, be considered at the outset.

Paying for it yourself, without using a solicitor

This will involve paying 'up front' for court fees and all the attendant costs of your claim or defence: telephone calls, photo-copying, letter writing, travel expenses to court and the cost of medical or other expert reports. There is also the matter of the time spent dealing with the case and attending court. Remember, you will not recover these costs unless the court orders the other party to pay them (or the other side agrees to pay them). The rules by which the court will order a sum to compensate the litigant-in-person for his time spent taking the case to court are set out on page 121.

Paying for yourself – using a solicitor to conduct the case

When you instruct a solicitor, you enter a contract with the firm. One of the first things that will be dealt with before he agrees to act for you, or you confirm your instruction, is the terms and

Highlight

The court may also decide that nobody should pay anyone else's costs, but that each party should bear his own.

conditions of acting. You may be given details of hourly rates charged by the various fee-earners and an estimate of the likely cost of funding your claim or defence. If you are unsure about the financial implications of instructing a solicitor, ask for clarification. The cost of court and experts fees will be included in the charge, as will the fees of a barrister instructed to act for you. Many solicitors will ask you to make a payment on account so that they can begin working on your behalf.

Legal expenses insurance

Many insurance policies such as car, health, professional or home will give you cover for legal expenses. This means that the insurance provider may provide in-house legal services in relation to your claim, and/or instruct a solicitor on your behalf. Look closely at the terms of your policy and discuss cover with your insurance company, to determine what cover entails and whether it is limited in any way. Most policies will require you to report the fact that you may have a claim within a short period of time (for example, within 14 or 21 days). You should check the policy for any such requirements and comply with them within the requisite period. If at the end of the case you are awarded your legal costs (or the other side agrees to pay them) the amount will be assessed in the normal way depending on the appropriate rules for Small Claims, Fast Track or Multi Track cases. The costs awarded will be paid. Even though you might not have actually paid the costs (because the insurer has paid them on your behalf) you will be awarded your costs, which should then be paid to the insurer.

Community Legal Services Funding (formerly Legal Aid)

On the 1st April 2000, the old Legal Aid system was officially replaced by Community Legal Services Funding, under the Access to Justice Act 1999. Neither claimants nor defendants may receive Community Legal Services Funding for claims arising from the negligent causing of injury, death or damage to property. Thus the bulk of personal injury claims will no longer be funded by the taxpayer (such as those arising out of road traffic accidents, or 'tripping-and-slipping' cases).

Community Legal Services Funding is still available for the legal costs of clinical negligence claims, or deliberately caused injuries such as assaults (battery), intentional causation of harm, or harassment. However, such funding will only be open to those in financial need (as defined in the regulations) and to those whose case merits funding under the regulations (as set out in the Funding Code). A solicitor will be able to advise whether a litigant qualifies for Community Legal Services Funding.

'No-win-no-fee' (conditional fee agreements)

Any glimpse at advertising hoardings or daytime television will show that there has been a development in this area of financing claims. It is central to government policy and goes hand-in-hand with the curtailing of public funding for many types of personal injury work.

A conditional fee agreement (a 'CFA') is an agreement between a solicitor and his client in which the solicitor agrees to provide advocacy or litigation services on a 'no-win-no-fee' basis. When the client is successful in obtaining a payment of damages from the other side he will have to pay the fee (which of course is probably recoverable from the other side as an award of 'costs') plus a percentage uplift called a 'success fee'. The success fee must be a percentage of the solicitor's fees and expenses in the case; the Law Society recommend an uplift of 25 per cent, but the statute sets a maximum of 100 per cent.

Getting free advice and representation

There are various organisations that provide free advice to litigants. Often this will take the form of initial advice on the merits of a claim and help with filling in forms. **Citizens Advice Bureaux** are staffed by lawyers and volunteers and can be found in town centres and sometimes at help desks in the courts. **Legal Advice Centres** serve a similar function and are staffed by qualified and trainee solicitors and barristers. It may be that in special cases a solicitors' firm, or barrister instructed through a solicitor, will agree to represent a litigant *pro bono*, in other words, for free. It may also be worth checking to see if the students at the law faculty of a local university or law college run a **student advice centre**.

Highlight

A conditional fee agreement (a 'CFA') is an agreement between a solicitor and his client in which the solicitor agrees to provide advocacy or litigation services on a 'no win, no fee' basis.

Representation by a 'Mckenzie friend'

Where the judge is satisfied that a litigant-in-person requires, in the interests of justice or for reasons of fairness, a lay adviser to assist him, then the litigant-in-person may have a 'Mckenzie friend' to help him at hearings in open court. The Mckenzie friend is not a lawyer, but is there for moral and practical support. In a Small Claims Track trial, and as long as the litigant is present, the lay adviser may actually present the case for the litigant.

Whom to sue?

Deciding who is responsible

First decide who is responsible for your injury, in law. You will have to analyse your case and think: who acted negligently? Who breached the contract? Chapter 1 of this guide discusses some common situations of 'liability'. You may have to do some fact-finding before you come to an answer. You may even have to obtain the opinion of an expert in the relevant field before you can pinpoint who has done wrong or caused you the injury. You may have to do some legal research into breaches of statutory duty. Most of the time, however, the question of liability will be easily answered. Do not forget, however, that you only have limited time to find out who is liable, and to bring a claim against him (see 'Is it too late to sue?' on page 63).

The next question: is there anyone else who may also be liable? There may be more than one person who is responsible for your injury. Not only do you have limited time in which to bring your claim, but the court may not allow you to bring a second claim against a different person relating to the same injury if the first one fails. Suing everyone at the same time in one claim also keeps down the costs.

Example

I am injured in a car accident which was caused by the negligent driving of two separate drivers.

It is sensible to claim against them both by naming them as first and second defendant (although I am not obliged to do so). If I

---

am successful against them both, the judge will decide how the damages are to be apportioned between them.

Example

I have a biopsy and the local health trust's pathology lab negligently fails to pick up the abnormality. I then move to a different health authority's area where my new GP negligently fails to pick up further warning signs resulting in additional and unnecessary complications and suffering.

I should sue both the pathologist and the GP. As both doctors are employed by their respective area health authorities, I should also sue the employers (see below).

Different types of defendant

Suing an individual's employer

Where an individual acts negligently 'in the course of his employment', the law holds his employer liable (responsible) for that negligence. This is called 'vicarious liability'. Thus, where the negligent person is employed by an individual, that individual will also be held liable for the negligence. Similarly, where a negligent employee is employed by a company or a firm that company or firm is vicariously liable for his negligence. The advantage of this rule is that often an employee will not be able to afford to pay any damages he is told to pay, whereas an employer is more likely to be able to do so (and will probably be insured against 'third party claims', such as yours). Because vicarious liability is parallel to actual liability and depends on the employee acting in the course of his employment, it is wise to sue both employer and employee.

Example

I am shopping in 'Sam's Greens' which is a greengrocer's shop owned and run by Sam Browne. Theresa Wilson, the shop assistant, negligently hits me with a crate of lettuces she is lifting.

Highlight

Where an individual acts negligently 'in the course of his employment', the law holds his employer liable (responsible) for that negligence.

Although Theresa Wilson is primarily liable, her employer is also liable, vicariously. Therefore, I should name 'Theresa Wilson' as first defendant, and 'Sam Browne trading as Sam's Greens' as second defendant.

Example

Theresa Wilson, driving on her way to work at 'Sam's Greens' negligently drives her car into me causing me injury.

In this example I should only name Theresa Wilson; her employer Sam Browne will not be liable as she was not acting 'in the course of her employment', but merely getting to work.

Example

Sam Browne employs Tina Smith as a driver to make deliveries of vegetables around the local area in a van. On one delivery round, Tina is involved in a road traffic accident in which I am injured.

I should sue Tina Smith (first defendant) and Sam Browne (second defendant) in this instance; Tina was negligent in the course of her employment.

Highlight

Often a person may be 'trading as' under a different name; if it is relevant to the case, for clarity, he should be sued under both names.

Suing an individual

Where the wrongdoer is an individual person, they should be sued as such. Often a person may be 'trading as' under a different name; if it is relevant to the case, for clarity, he should be sued under both names.

Example

I am injured by Sam Browne in a car accident. He is driving to work as a greengrocer at the time, where he trades under the name of 'Sam's Greens'.

In this instance the fact that he is a greengrocer trading under a different name is irrelevant to his negligent driving. I should sue him in the name of 'Sam Browne'.

Example

I am injured at Sam Browne's greengrocers, slipping on a piece of cabbage leaf negligently left on the floor. The greengrocer's is called 'Sam's Greens'.

Here Sam's job and trading name are relevant to the case and it is appropriate to sue him in the name of 'Sam Browne, trading as 'Sam's Greens''.

Claims against companies

In law, companies are separate 'legal entities'; as soon as a company is 'incorporated' it becomes a creature distinct from the people who run it. Thus, a company can owe a duty of care and can enter contracts. When things go wrong, therefore, a company may be held liable to those who suffer. Of course, it is usually the officers or employees of the company who have done the wrongful act, but it is the company that is held responsible.

You will be able to tell if you are dealing with a company because the letters 'plc' or 'Ltd' usually appear as part of the name. The letterhead used by a company will usually reveal the 'registered address' to where correspondence may be sent. If in doubt, it is possible to find out if a 'company' is in fact incorporated, by doing a search of the register at Companies House (for a small fee).

> **Highlight**
>
> It is usually the officers or employees of the company who have done the wrongful act, but it is the company that is held responsible.

Example

Sam Browne has decided to form a limited company to carry on his expanding greengrocer's business. On the 4th July 2000, 'Sam's Greens Limited' is incorporated. On the 6th September 2000, I trip over some badly laid flooring in his shop and injure myself.

My claim should be against 'Sam's Greens Ltd'.

Claims against firms or other partnerships

A firm or partnership, unlike a company, is not a legal entity separate from its members. An individual partner will therefore be personally liable:

(a) for his own wrongful acts; and

(b) for the wrongful acts of his co-partners committed in the normal course of the firm's business; and

(c) for the wrongful acts of the employees of the partnership committed whilst acting in the course of their employment.

Where the partners are defendants under (b) or (c) above they are sued in the name of the firm (i.e. the claimants are expressed to be ''Thompson, Thompson and Smythe', a firm'.) Only those partners who were partners at the time of the act complained of will be held liable.

Example

Gary is a partner in a firm of solicitors. Driving on his way to work one morning he negligently causes a collision in which another driver was injured.

He is personally liable for his own negligence; however, as in driving to work he was not acting in the course of the firm's business, his co-partners will not be liable for his negligence.

Example

A client visits Gary's firm's offices for an appointment. Unfortunately, she trips on a rickety stair and injures herself.

In this instance the partners in the firm will be held liable 'jointly and singly' for their unsafe premises. This is because the premises are part of their business.

Claims against unincorporated associations

There are many situations where people join together in an enterprise without forming a company. Examples might include a sports club or charity or other association or club. Such clubs are made up of all the members, and under the law are only a collection of individuals. Care should be taken when deciding whom to sue; are all the members of the club liable, or only some members? If the wrongdoing was the fault of certain members acting on their own, then they should be sued as individuals. If, however, the wrongdoing was something that every member of the club could be held liable for, it would be unwieldy to name each and every one of them. In this circumstance, the law will allow one or more persons to act as 'representatives' of all the other members so as to defend the action. If damages are awarded against the representatives, they may recover the money from the other members.

Example

I slip on defective flooring on an ill-lit flight of stairs at a local badminton club. The club consists of 300 members and the building is owned by the club in the name of the captain Hugh MacKay.

I should make an application to the court under Civil Practice Rule 19.6 to name Hugh MacKay as a 'representative' of all of the members of the Club (a representative order). This is because the court will only make a person represent others if all the people represented would defend the action in the same way. In this example, all the people represented would raise the same defence to the action.

Example

A leading member of a local political party and a few of his fellow members begin to harass me when I announce my intention to leave the party and join a rival group. This harassment causes me a great deal of anxiety and stress.

I should sue the individuals harassing me in their own right. This case is not appropriate for an application that the leading member is made a representative of all the other members of the club. The members of the club do not have the 'same interest' in defending the case. This may be because some members of the club might defend the action on the basis that they knew nothing of the harassment and had nothing to do with it; others might have a very different defence, such as what they did not amount to harassment; some of the members might decide that they have a good chance of winning their defence, and fight on, whilst another defendant or defendants might consider my case so strong against them that they want to settle out of court. Thus it is fairer to let everyone have a chance of defending the case against them. The individuals responsible should be sued, and it is unlikely that one or more members will be ordered by the court to 'represent' all the other members.

Claims against children

A child can be sued for personal injuries caused by him, although a child defendant must have a litigation friend acting on his behalf (see 'Can I bring a claim?' on page 80). It is worth noting, however, that children (by virtue of age and inexperience) are not expected to have the same awareness of danger or the consequences of their actions that adults have. A great deal will depend on what a reasonably sensible child of the defendant's age would have done.

Correcting mistakenly-named parties

It is essential that the parties are named correctly; court orders will bind those named. Thus, the party issuing a claim must:

- identify the correct party; *and*

- name them correctly.

The defendant should draw attention to any inaccuracies of identification or nomenclature as soon as he realises the mistake.

Example

I am involved in a road traffic accident with Ian Reed, a lorry driver who works for a company. My claim form names Ian Reed and 'CAB Transport Ltd' (registered office in Leeds) as defendants. Ian Reed's defence denies that he works for CAB Transport Ltd, and states that he is employed by ABC

Transport Ltd of Carlisle. CAB Transport Ltd's Defence denies employing Ian Reed.

It is clear that I have named a wrong party. I should apply to the court to discontinue the case against CAB Transport Ltd, and at the same time apply to substitute ABC Transport Ltd as a defendant.

Example

I am involved in a road traffic accident with a person whose name I take to be Sarah-Jane Mitchland, living at 14 Ormah Road, London. I name her as defendant in my claim form and other court documents. At the first hearing it becomes clear that her name is in fact Sarah-Joan Mitcham. She lives at 14 Ormah Road and accepts that she was involved in the accident, although she denies it was her fault.

This is a case of simply getting the name wrong. I should ask the court for permission to amend the claim form and statements of case. This is done by filling in an 'Application Notice' form (see 'Preparation for trial' on page 101).

Can I bring a claim?

The question 'Can I bring a claim?' really begs two further questions: (a) is the defendant liable to me? and (b) do I have the capacity to conduct a case through the courts? The first is really a question of whether or not you have a claim in law, known as *locus standi* or standing. The answer to (a) therefore, will be found in 'Personal injuries arising from negligence, breach of contract or nuisance' on page 64. The second question is a matter of practicality rather than law. Usually, the person who suffered the injury brings the claim. However, certain claimants cannot act for themselves: there are special rules for child claimants, the mentally ill and the deceased. The section below deals with the answers to question (b).

Children: 0–17 years

Unless the court orders otherwise, a child cannot conduct litigation. Instead, although the child will be named as a *party* in the normal way, a 'litigation friend' acts in his interests and make all necessary decisions connected with the litigation (e.g. instructing a lawyer, conducting negotiations and filling forms, etc.). The appointment of a litigation friend automatically ceases upon the child's 18th birthday (unless the 'child' is also mentally disordered and therefore also a 'patient' for the time being), and the 18-year-old must let the other parties know the situation, and indicate if he intends to continue with the case.

In some circumstances, depending on the age of the child, and the nature of the claim, etc., the court may feel that there is no need for a litigation friend and order accordingly. A child may apply to the court for an order himself (see 'Applications in the period before trial' on page 109).

For discussion on how to become a litigation friend please see below.

Other rules for claims involving children

Damages awarded to a child will usually be 'paid into court' and invested by the court on the child's behalf until he reaches the age of 18. However, the court may make different arrangements as appropriate (for example, allowing a payment out at an earlier time).

Additionally, any out-of-court settlement (see 'Settling 'out of court" on page 123) involving a child party must be approved by the court. The judge will look at the terms of settlement to see that the child's interests have been protected.

Mentally disordered persons

A person suffering from a mental disorder which renders him incapable of managing his own affairs can be a party in litigation. However, the case must be conducted on his behalf by a 'litigation friend'. Where a person is capable of managing his own affairs at the start of a case, but later becomes mentally ill to the extent that he can no longer manage his own affairs, a litigation friend should be appointed to continue the conduct of the case. Conversely,

Highlight

A person suffering from a mental disorder which renders him incapable of managing his own affairs can be a party in litigation.

where a person who is conducting litigation by a litigation friend becomes well and capable of managing his own affairs, there is no need for a litigation friend to act. The court will make an order terminating the appointment of the litigation friend.

Becoming a litigation friend

Part 21 of the Civil Procedural Rules governs how a person becomes a litigation friend. The court may order a person to be a litigation friend on behalf of a child or patient. The court may also make an order allowing a child to take or defend proceedings without a litigation friend (which will mean that he can instruct a lawyer or act as a litigant-in-person).

Where the court has not ordered someone to be a litigation friend, an authorised person under the Mental Health Act 1983 (in the case of 'patients' only) or a volunteer layman (often a friend or relative) may become a litigation friend. Any adult who is not a 'patient' may be a litigation friend. However, the litigation friend must:

- be able to conduct proceedings fairly and competently;

- have no 'conflict of interest' with the child or patient (see below);

- promise to the court (undertake) to pay any costs which the child or patient is ordered to pay during or at the end of the case.

A 'conflict of interest' is where two people have different interests in the way a case is managed, or in the outcome of a claim.

Example

Tommy is injured when his mother drives her car negligently into a tree. He wants to bring a claim for compensation and a family friend suggests that his mother should be his litigation friend.

The answer is that his mother cannot be his litigation friend. Tommy's mother has a conflict of interest with him because she will be the defendant. She may be wanting to deny the claim or admit the claim and pay the minimum she needs to in damages to him. Since Tommy's 'interest' is to prove that his mother drove negligently and obtain the maximum in damages from her insurers, his interest is directly opposed to hers.

Highlight

There is, in theory, no limit to the number of claimants that can bring an action against a defendant or defendants in a single claim.

Multiple claimants: suing as individuals in a single claim

There is, in theory, no limit to the number of claimants that can bring an action against a defendant or defendants in a single claim. For ease of administration and in the interests of fairness it may be appropriate to order separate trials, or make one or more claimants represent the others (see 'Multiple claimants: suing through a representative', below) or order that claims are dealt with together (see 'Multiple claimants: group litigation', below).

Multiple claimants: suing through a representative (by a representative order)

Where a group of potential claimants has a common grievance against a common defendant (or defendants), the court may decide that one or more of the group may 'represent' others, so as to limit the litigation and costs. However, this sort of order is unlikely to be made in personal injury litigation because few claimants will have the same 'interest' as another.

Multiple claimants: group litigation (by a group litigation order)

Sometimes, a group of potential claimants will have cases that raise common or related issues of fact or law. Where individuals begin separate cases (sometimes in different courts) the court can make a group litigation order, providing that all the cases be managed together.

The first step in litigation: 'pre-action protocols'

'Pre-action protocols' were introduced by the Woolf reforms in April 1999. The aim was to increase the likelihood of early settlement by promoting increased contact between the parties, better and earlier investigation of the claim and earlier and wider exchange of information between the parties about the claim. If matters do not settle then it is hoped that the path through the courts to trial will be quicker and more efficient than in the 'bad old days'. The spirit of the Woolf reforms discourages taking the opposite side by surprise or other such frowned-upon tactical behaviour.

Essentially, the pre-action protocols are lists of steps that should be taken by the parties (together with time limits for taking them) before the claimant issues a claim. They are designed to be used particularly with Fast Track cases, but the court will expect parties in Multi Track cases to comply with the spirit of the protocols, if not the letter. Co-operation in case preparation is expected under the new regime.

Failure to comply with the protocols

The court may take into account the failure of a party to comply with either the whole of a pre-action protocol, or the failure to comply with a particular step prescribed by a pre-action protocol when considering costs (see 'Costs' on page 119). It is therefore important to draw the court's attention to any such failure by the opposing party. However, minor breaches are unlikely to attract much criticism. Where a party was *disadvantaged* by the other's failure to comply, however, the court may wish to act upon that failure.

The protocol: personal injury claims

Step 1 The proposed claimant sends each proposed defendant two copies of a letter of claim; see Appendix 5 for specimen letter, which should be adapted to fit the circumstances of the case and in particular should:

a) set out a clear summary of the facts;

b) give a brief indication of the nature of the injuries;

c) make an indication of the nature and amount of financial loss suffered; and

d) ask for details of the proposed defendant's insurer.

Step 2 Within 21 days (of the letter of claim's date of posting) the proposed defendant(s) should:

a) pass the letter of claim to his insurance company, if he has one;

b) acknowledge receiving the letter of claim; and

c) give details of his insurers (if he has insurance for the particular type of case, for example compulsory road traffic insurance).

Step 3 The proposed defendant has a maximum of three calendar months after his letter of acknowledgement to investigate the claim. By the end of that period he should send to the proposed claimant his **letter of reply**

a) admitting the claim; or

b) denying liability; or

c) admitting liability but asserting 'contributory negligence'.

If liability is denied, the letter of reply should enclose any relevant documents which have a bearing on the case. If contributory negligence is asserted by the proposed defendant, he should specify his reasons in the letter of reply and enclose any relevant documentation. (For a discussion, see 'Contributory negligence' on page 51 for a discussion on disclosure of documents see 'Fast and Multi Track directions' on page 103).

Step 4 The proposed claimant should send to the proposed defendant *as soon as practicable* a **'schedule of special damages'**, if not before the proposed defendant has replied, then as soon as practicable after he has denied liability. A sample schedule of special damages can be found in 'Claimant: issuing a claim' on page 92.

Step 5 The proposed claimant will normally wish to **instruct an expert** (usually a medical specialist in the relevant field, but other professionals may be relevant, too) before issuing the claim. Certainly, he will have to have one ready when he issues his personal injury claim. The expert must be selected according to the method laid down in the rules.

The claimant gives the proposed defendant the name (or names) of suitable experts. Within 14 days, the defendant should agree with the proposed expert, or outline his objections to any of them. If no agreement can be agreed as to whom should be instructed, each party may instruct their own medical expert and the court will later decide if the parties have acted reasonably in failing to agree on whom should be instructed. Note that the expert(s) will need to look at relevant documentation, such as medical records, and conduct an examination, such as a site view, or medical examination of the claimant.

Step 6 The claimant issues the claim (see 'Claimant: issuing a claim' on page 89). Note that this must be within the limitation period (see 'Is it too late to sue?' on page 63 – it may be necessary to apply to the court for an extension of time).

The protocol: clinical disputes/negligence claims

This protocol differs slightly from the personal injury protocol, because it is tailored to the particular circumstances out of which such disputes arise. At the heart of a clinical dispute is a broken professional relationship between the healthcare worker and the patient. There are also disciplinary issues and sensitivities, involving both hospital/health trust and the relevant professional body (such as the General Medical Council). The protocol tries to foster openness at an early stage, encourage early investigation, promote early disclosure of medical records, facilitate resolution and discourage weak claims or defences from dragging on.

The protocol is divided into two parts;

(a) the 'initial stages' which impose 'good practice commitments' on the patient and the healthcare provider; and

(b) the 'protocol stages' which outline a series of steps which are designed to achieve the early resolution of the dispute and the efficient preparation for trial.

Initial stages

1. The patient and his advisers should report any concerns and dissatisfactions to the healthcare provider, as soon as is reasonable in the circumstances. This enables the healthcare provider to offer clinical advice if appropriate, and to advise (admit) if anything has gone wrong.

2. The healthcare provider should tell the patient (i.e. without being asked) if there has been a 'serious adverse outcome'. He should provide an oral or written explanation of what has happened and, where appropriate, offer further treatment to rectify the problem, an apology, changes in procedure and compensation.

3. The patient and his advisers should consider all routes open to him: request for an explanation, a meeting, lodging a complaint, alternative dispute resolution (See 'Settling 'out of court'' on page 123) and negotiation, as well as litigation. The healthcare worker should advise the patient of such options available to him.

Protocol steps

1. The patient should **ask to see copies of his medical records**, being specific about which records are required (i.e. relating to a particular procedure) and giving an indication to the healthcare provider about what has gone wrong (see the approved specimen form for this request at Appendix 4). There is a charge for this – currently £10, plus photocopying and postage costs.

2. The healthcare provider should provide the records within 40 days and explain promptly where there is a problem in complying and give details of how the problem is being resolved.

3. If the healthcare provider fails to provide the records or an explanation described above, the patient may **apply to the court for pre-action disclosure** (see 'Applications in the period before trial', page 109).

4. Patient and healthcare provider will need to consider whether or not to **instruct expert(s)** so that the following issues can be analysed:

    - whether or not a healthcare worker has been negligent; and/or

    - the patient's condition and prognosis; and/or

    - the value of the claim (i.e. the likely damages).

    The expert(s) may be instructed by each party, by one party with the agreement of the other, or jointly, as appropriate.

5. Where there is no resolution of the dispute, the patient sends the healthcare provider a **letter of claim**. This should contain a clear summary of the facts relied upon, an indication of the negligence alleged, a description of the claimant's injuries, present condition and prognosis and an outline of financial losses suffered and expected. A specimen letter, which should be adapted to fit the circumstances is included at Appendix 4. No claim should be issued for three months, to allow the healthcare provider time to make further investigations and consider their position.

6. The proposed defendant (the healthcare provider) should send to the patient an **acknowledgement letter** within 14 days of receiving it, identifying whom is dealing with the matter.

7. The proposed defendant should send the patient a **letter of response** within three months (it is not clear if this time limit is three months from the day the letter was *posted*, or three months from the date the proposed defendant *received* it; but in practice this should not make much difference). The letter of response should state (and give reasons):

    - *if the claim* is admitted;

    - if part of the claim is admitted;

    - if the claim is denied (specifying what issues are disputed).

8. If there has been no settlement by this stage, the claimant may issue his claim.

Claimant: issuing a claim

A claim begins when it is 'issued' by the court. The claimant asks the court to do this by filling in a Claim Form Form N1 and giving details of the claim in a Particulars of Claim. He must also include a copy of any **medical expert's report** he intends to rely on (see 'The first step in litigation: pre-action protocols' above) and a **schedule of past and future expenses and losses claimed** (also known as a 'schedule of special damages').

Filling in the Claim Form

The Claim Form (Form N1) can be obtained from the court or from the court service website www.courtservice.gov.uk. It comes with comprehensive and easy-to-understand notes to help you fill it in. See example on page 90. You must then make copies:

- one for the court (the original);
- one for *each* defendant;
- one for your own records.

Schedule of special damages

A schedule of special damages is a document that forms part of the Particulars of Claim. It is designed to show the defendant how much you are claiming for the expenses incurred already. It can be updated before trial if necessary. For advice on what can be claimed see ' Compensation for financial loss and expenses up to the date of trial or settlement' on page 134. An example schedule of special damages is shown on page 92.

Issuing the claim

Retaining a copy of the Claim Form and enclosures (see checklist below), send or take the documents to the relevant court. Do not forget to pay the issue fee! The court will issue it by stamping its seal on the documents together with the day's date.

Form N1 (Claim Form)

If your claim is for more than £50,000 you may issue in the High Court or in the County Court. If the total claimed (not including interest or costs) is less than £50,000, you may only bring a personal injury case in the County Court.

Where: If you are suing in the High Court you should bring a claim in your local District Registry, or if there is not one, the Royal Courts of Justice in London. If you are suing in the County Court, you may begin in any County Court but the case may be transferred to the most convenient court.

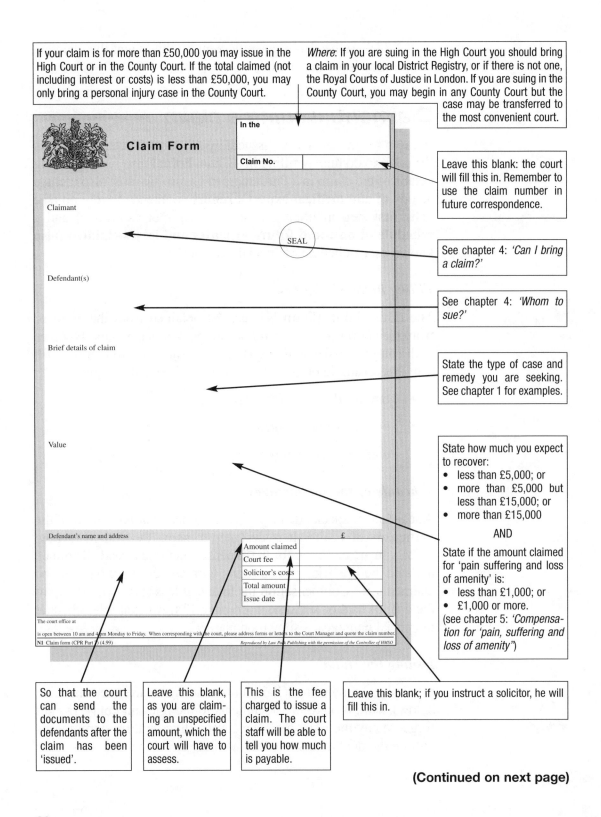

Claim Form

In the

Claim No.

Leave this blank: the court will fill this in. Remember to use the claim number in future correspondence.

Claimant

SEAL

See chapter 4: *'Can I bring a claim?'*

Defendant(s)

See chapter 4: *'Whom to sue?'*

Brief details of claim

State the type of case and remedy you are seeking. See chapter 1 for examples.

Value

State how much you expect to recover:
- less than £5,000; or
- more than £5,000 but less than £15,000; or
- more than £15,000

AND

State if the amount claimed for 'pain suffering and loss of amenity' is:
- less than £1,000; or
- £1,000 or more.

(see chapter 5: *'Compensation for 'pain, suffering and loss of amenity'*)

Defendant's name and address

£

Amount claimed	
Court fee	
Solicitor's costs	
Total amount	
Issue date	

The court office at

is open between 10 am and 4 pm Monday to Friday. When corresponding with the court, please address forms or letters to the Court Manager and quote the claim number.

N1 Claim form (CPR Part 7) (4.99)   *Reproduced by Law Pack Publishing with the permission of the Controller of HMSO*

So that the court can send the documents to the defendants after the claim has been 'issued'.

Leave this blank, as you are claiming an unspecified amount, which the court will have to assess.

This is the fee charged to issue a claim. The court staff will be able to tell you how much is payable.

Leave this blank; if you instruct a solicitor, he will fill this in.

(Continued on next page)

Form N1 (Claim Form) *(continued)*

For sample particulars see Appendix 1.

You can:

(a) write your particulars in the box; or

(b) attach your particulars to the Claim Form on a separate piece of paper (with a heading which shows: the claim number; the name of the court; the names of the parties; and service; or

(c) state that particulars will follow. Send the defendant(s) your particulars set out as (b) above, to arrive within 14 days of the issue date.

If you sign a statement of truth without believing the facts are true, you are committing a 'contempt of court' for which you may be tried and punished by imprisonment.

Fill this in as appropriate.

	Claim No.

Particulars of Claim (attached)(to follow)

Statement of Truth
*(I believe)(The Claimant believes) that the facts stated in these particulars of claim are true.
*I am duly authorised by the claimant to sign this statement

Full name

Name of claimant's solicitor's firm

signed ——————————————— position or office held ————————
*(Claimant)(Litigation friend)(Claimant's solicitor) (if signing on behalf of firm or company)
*delete as appropriate

Claimant's or claimant's solicitor's address to which documents or payments should be sent if different from overleaf including (if appropriate) details of DX, fax or e-mail.

Example schedule of special damages

CASE NO: 758FK947

IN THE ANYTOWN COUNTY COURT

BETWEEN

MISS HARRIET CHURCH   <u>Claimant</u>

and

MRS RACHEL GOLDSTEIN   <u>Defendant</u>

<u>SCHEDULE OF SPECIAL DAMAGES</u>

[*List here all the expenses e.g.*:

analgesic tablets (3 per week for 4 weeks at £1.89 each) –   £22.68

4 visits to consultant at Anyshire County Hospital

round trip = 32 miles @36p per mile –   £46.08

net lost earnings: 1 week beginning 19th August 2000 –   £75.00

Total   £143.76]

CHECKLIST

❑ Claim Form, signed and verified;

❑ Particulars of Claim, if contained in a separate document, signed and verified;

❑ Medical expert's report;

❑ Schedule of special damages, signed and verified;

❑ Court fee (£20–£400, depending on the value of the claim; the court will advise you of the amount payable).

'Service' of the claim

The court will send the defendant(s) copies of the Claim Form and other documents and a 'Response Pack'. If you are providing the Particulars of Claim separately from the Claim Form, remember to send it directly to the court and to each defendant in time (see above).

Defendant: how to deal with the Response Pack

Highlight

Do not ignore the Claim Form; it will not go away!

The Response Pack contains a number of forms and helpful explanatory notes. Only one (or possibly two) of the forms will be relevant to your situation, so choose which you use with great care. Do not ignore the Claim Form; it will not go away! If you do nothing the claimant may apply to the court for 'judgment in default' (see 'Cutting litigation short' page 95) and either order you to pay a sum or list the case for a hearing to decide what sum you will have to pay.

Will you:

• Admit liability for the whole claim? – file (i.e. send to the court) an 'admission' Form N9C *within 14 days of receiving the Particulars of Claim*. This form enables you to also offer an amount of money which the claimant will decide to reject or accept. The chapter 'How compensation is calculated' on page 129 discusses how to calculate how much a claim is worth. 'Settling 'out of court'' on page 123 gives advice on how to calculate how much to offer.

- Deny liability? – file and serve a 'defence' Form N9D *within 14 days of receiving the Particulars of Claim.*

- Admit liability for part of the claim, but deny some of it? – file and serve both admission Form N9C and defence Form N9D – *within 14 days of receiving the Particulars of Claim.*

- Need a bit more time to investigate the claim? – file an 'acknowledgement of service' Form N9 *within 14 days of receiving the Particulars of Claim* and file and serve a 'defence' Form N9D *within a further 14 days.*

Choosing whether to admit or deny liability

What is the claimant's case? You will need to read the Claim Form carefully to discover what the claimant is claiming. If the pre-action protocols have been followed, you will already know quite a lot about the claimant's case, and your own.

What is my case? Consider if you have a defence to the claim (see 'Defences' on page 47). You will probably be able to agree some facts; for example, you might agree with the claimant that you were both involved in an accident on 8th December 1999. The more that is agreed between the parties the less there is for the judge to decide and the more focus there will be on important issues that are really in dispute. You will see that the sample defence paragraphs in Appendix 2 show how to deal with parts of the Particulars of Claim that are agreed, or 'not admitted' or denied. It is important to deal in this way with each allegation separately where it helps clarity. The defence should set out your version of events clearly. You will have to also tell the court if you accept the sums claimed as 'special damages' (losses and expenses claimed by the claimant up to the date of trial, i.e. not his future losses).

It is possible to agree certain matters without prejudicing your defence.

Highlight

The more that is agreed between the parties the less there is for the judge to decide and the more focus there will be on important issues which are really in dispute.

Example

The claimant claims that her car cost £3,005.74 to repair. She provides an original receipt from the garage that repaired it to back up her claim. Although you do not accept that your driving caused the accident and blame her driving (i.e. you are denying liability), you do not wish to dispute the cost of repairing her car as the damage was caused in the accident; it was reasonable of her to have her car repaired in the circumstances and the amount charged by the garage was also reasonable. Your defence can therefore contain the phrase 'without prejudice to the defendant's denial of liability the amount of the repair cost is admitted'.

Counter-schedule of special damages

If a 'schedule of special damages' has been served and you wish to dispute some or all of the items, you should set out your responses in a counter-schedule. This follows the same pattern as the schedule of special damages and is designed for everyone to see at a glance what is agreed and what is still in dispute. You should make it clear if you agree or disagree with:

- the type of damage claimed;
- the amount claimed for a particular type of damage (is it a reasonable amount?).

Filling in the admission: Form N9C

See example on page 96.

Filling in the defence/counterclaim: Form N9D

See example on page 98.

Cutting litigation short; when can a trial be avoided?

Highlight

One shortcut avoiding full trial is available where the case put forward by one of the parties is so weak that it is bound to fail at trial.

Summary judgment: when the claim/defence is weak

Once the claim and defences have been filed, the preparation for trial begins (see below). However, one shortcut avoiding full trial is available where the case put forward by one of the parties is so weak that it is bound to fail at trial. A party, either the claimant or

Form N9C (Admission)

Admission (specified amount, non-money and return of goods claims)

- Before completing this form please read the notes for guidance attached to the claim form. If necessary provide details on a separate sheet, add the claim number and attach it to this form.
- If you are not an individual, you should ensure that you provide sufficient details about the assets and liabilities of your firm, company or corporation to support any offer of payment made.

In the	
Claim No.	
Claimant (including ref.)	
Defendant	

In non-money claims only

☐ I admit liability for the whole claim
(Complete section 11)

In return of goods cases only

Are the goods still in your possession?
☐ Yes ☐ No

Part A Response to claim *(tick one box only)*

☐ I admit liability for the whole claim but want the court to decide the amount I should pay / value of the goods

OR

☐ I admit liability for the claim and offer to pay [   ] in satisfaction of the claim
(Complete part B and sections 1–11)

Part B How are you going to pay the amount you have admitted? *(tick one box only)*

☐ I offer to pay on (date) [   ]

OR

☐ I cannot pay the amount immediately because *(state reason)*

[   ]

AND

I offer to pay by instalments of £ [   ]
per (week)(month)
starting *(date)* [   ]

1 Personal details

Surname [   ]

Forename [   ]

☐ Mr ☐ Mrs ☐ Miss ☐ Ms
☐ Married ☐ Single ☐ Other *(specify)*

Age [   ]

Address [   ]

Postcode [   ]

Tel. no. [   ]

2 Dependants *(people you look after financially)*

Number of children in each age group

Under 11 [ ] 11-15 [ ] 16-17 [ ] 18 & over [ ]

Other dependants [   ]
(give details)

3 Employment

☐ **I am employed as a** [   ]
My employer is [   ]

Jobs other than
main job *(give details)* [   ]

☐ **I am self employed as a** [   ]
Annual turnover is .... £ [   ]

☐ **I am not** in arrears with my national insurance contributions, income tax and VAT

☐ **I am** in arrears and I owe .... £ [   ]

Give details of:
(a) contracts and other work in hand
(b) any sums due for work done

☐ **I have been unemployed for** [years   months]

☐ **I am a pensioner**

4 Bank account and savings

☐ **I have a bank account**
The account is in credit by ...... £ [   ]
The account is overdrawn by ... £ [   ]

☐ **I have a savings or building society account**
The amount in the account is ...... £ [   ]

5 Residence

I live in
☐ my own property ☐ lodgings
☐ jointly owned house ☐ rented property
☐ council accommodation

N9C Admission (unspecified amount and non-money claims) (8.99)   Reproduced by Law Pack Publishing with the permission of the Controller of HMSO

Tick this box if you admit liability but want the court to decide at a hearing how much the damages and costs will be.

Tick this box if you admit liability and want to offer to pay the claim. If the claimant does not accept the amount, a hearing will be fixed so that the court can decide how much you should pay.

Parts B1–11 need only be filled in if you are offering to settle.

(Continued on next page)

6 Income

	£	per
My usual take home pay *(including overtime, commission, bonuses etc)*	£	per
Income support	£	per
Child benefit(s)	£	per
Other state benefit(s)	£	per
My pension(s)	£	per
Others living in my home give me	£	per
Other income *(give details below)*		
	£	per
	£	per
	£	per
Total income	**£**	**per**

Parts B1–11 need only be filled in if you are offering to settle.

7 Expenses

(Do not include any payments made by other members of the household out of their own income)

I have regular expenses as follows:

	£	per
Mortgage *(including second mortgage)*	£	per
Rent	£	per
Council tax	£	per
Gas	£	per
Electricity	£	per
Water charges	£	per
TV rental and licence	£	per
HP repayments	£	per
Mail order	£	per
Housekeeping, food, school meals	£	per
Travelling expenses	£	per
Children's clothing	£	per
Maintenance payments	£	per
Others *(not court orders or credit debts listed in sections 9 and 10)*		
	£	per
	£	per
	£	per
Total expenses	**£**	**per**

8 Priority debts

(This section is for arrears only. Do not include regular expenses listed in section 7)

	£	per
Rent arrears	£	per
Mortgage arrears	£	per
Council tax/Community Charge arrears	£	per
Water charges arrears	£	per
Fuel debts: Gas	£	per
Electricity	£	per
Other	£	per
Maintenance arrears	£	per
Others *(give details below)*		
	£	per
	£	per
Total priority debts	**£**	**per**

9 Court orders

Court	Claim No.	£	per

Total court order instalments	**£**	**per**

Of the payments above, I am behind with payments to *(please list)*

10 Credit debts

Loans and credit card devts *(please list)*

	£	per
	£	per
	£	per

Of the payments above, I am behind with payments to *(please list)*

11 Declaration

I declare that the details I have given above are true to the best of my knowledge

Signed

Position or office held *(if signing on behalf of firm or company)*

Date

You must fill in this box. However, making a declaration of truth without an honest belief in the truth of the statements in the document is a 'contempt of court' which is punishable by imprisonment.

Form N9D (Defence and Counterclaim)

Defence and Counterclaim
(unspecified amount, non-money and return of goods claims)

- Fill in this form if you wish to dispute all or part of the claim and/or make a claim against the claimant (a counterclaim)
- You have a listed number of days to complete and return this form to the court.
- Before completing this form, please read the notes for guidance attached to the claim form.
- Please ensure that all the boxes at the top right of this form are completed. You can obtain the correct names and number from the claim form. The court cannot trace your case without this information.

How to fill in this form
- Set out your defence in section 1. If necessary continue on a separate piece of paper making sure that the claim number is clearly shown on it. In your defence you must state which allegations in the particulars of claim you deny and your reasons for doing so. **If you fail to deny an allegation it may be taken that you admit it.**
- If you dispute only some of the allegations you must
  – specify which you admit and which you deny; and
  – give your own version of events if different from the claimant's.

In the	
Claim No.	
Claimant (including ref.)	
Defendant	

- If the claim is for money and you dispute the claimant's statement of value, you must say why and if possible give your own statement of value.
- If you wish to make a claim against the claimant (a counterclaim) complete section 2.
- Complete and sign section 3 before returning this form.

Where to send this form
- send or take this form immediately to the court at the address given on the claim form.
- Keep a copy of the claim form and the defence form.

Community Legal Service Fund (CLSF)
You may qualify for assistance from the CLSF (this used to be called 'legal aid') to meet some or all of your legal costs. Ask about the CLSF at any county court office or any information or help point which displays this logo.

Community Legal Service

1. Defence

> For sample defence paragraphs, see Appendix 2.

> Remember, even if you have sent your defence, you can make an 'offer of settlement' – if it is made 'without prejudice', the judge does not hear about it, and therefore if it is not accepted, the trial continues. See 'Settling 'out of court'', page 123.

(Continued on next page)

Form N9D (Defence and Counterclaim) *(continued)*

Defence (continued)

Claim No. [   ]

A counterclaim works in the same way a 'claim' does. If you have suffered a personal injury you will be asking for an unspecified amount. Therefore leave this blank.

2. If you wish to make a claim against the claimant (a counterclaim)

If your claim is for a specific sum of money, how much are you claiming? £ [   ]

- To start your counterclaim, you will have to pay a fee. Court staff will tell you how much you have to pay.

- You may not be able to make a counterclaim where the claimant is the Crown (e.g. a Government Department). Ask at your local county court office for further information.

My claim is for *(please specify)*

For example: 'damages for personal injuries and consequential losses arising from a car accident'. See chapter 1 for sample 'brief details of claim' arising in various situations.

What are your reasons for making the counterclaim?
If you need to continue on a separate sheet put the claim number in the top right hand corner

3. Signed
(To be signed by you or by your solicitor or litigation friend)

*(I believe)(The defendant believes) that the facts stated in this form are true. *I am duly authorised by the defendant to sign this statement

*delete as appropriate

Position or office held
(if signing on behalf of firm or company)

Date

Give an address to which notices about this case can be sent to you

Postcode

Tel. no.

if applicable

fax no.

DX no.

e-mail

If you sign this not believing that the facts stated are true, you will be in 'contempt of court' which is punishable by, amongst other things, imprisonment.

defendant, can ask the court to look at the evidence filed and 'give judgment' there and then at the preliminary hearing.

An **Application Notice** (Form N244, available from the court office) should be completed, and evidence, including a witness statement, may be attached. The other party may file evidence in response before the hearing.

At the hearing, the judge will read the statements of case (the Claim, the Particulars of Claim and the Defence), the application notice and any witness statements. He will then decide (where the application is brought by the claimant) whether the defendant has no real prospect of successfully defending the claim and whether is no other reason for having a trial of the dispute. Where the application is made by the defendant, the judge must decide whether the claimant has a real prospect of succeeding on the claim.

The judge will not try to decide 'who is telling the truth'; that is a decision which is only suitable for trial.

In some circumstances the judge may decide, without being asked, that the claim or defence should be 'struck out'. This may be because the papers filed by the claimant or defendant do not show that there is a reason for bringing or defending the claim. Alternatively, a judge may decide that one of the parties is bound to fail at trial and there is no other reason for trial. In that case, the parties will be told to attend a hearing or take other steps (such as amend their statement of case, or provide more information).

Failure to file a defence: the 'default judgment'

Where the defendant fails to respond to the claim by filing a defence or an 'acknowledgement of service' and defence within the time allowed (see 'Defendant: how to deal with the response pack' above) the claimant can ask the court to 'enter judgment'. There is no need for a hearing of this application. The effect of obtaining a default judgment is that the defendant is held liable for the claim. The court will decide how much damages should be paid at a 'disposal hearing'. At such a hearing, only evidence as to the amount of damages will be heard or read. The court will not re-open the issue of liability at the hearing. Directions for the preparation of the disposal hearing will by given in the normal way (see 'Preparation for trial', page 101).

Applying for a default judgment

Use Form N205B (Notice of Issue (unspecified amount) and Request for Judgment), which the court will have sent you when your claim was issued. Alternatively you can use Form N227 (Request for Default Judgment).

Note that if your claim is against a 'child' or a 'patient' or your spouse, you must apply for a default judgment by making an application to the court using an Application Notice **Form N244**; (see 'Applications in the period before trial', page 109). In these situations, there will be a hearing of the application for judgment.

Preparation for trial ━━━━━━━

Allocation of the case to a trial 'track'

Once a defence has been filed at court, the court sends each party an allocation questionnaire. This must be completed and returned within a particular time.

The court will allocate the case to the most appropriate 'track'. The **Small Claims Track** is designed for cases where the claimant's claim for 'pain, suffering and loss of amenity' is worth less than £1,000 and the total damages claimed are less than £5,000. Only the most minor injuries will therefore qualify for this Track. The pre-action protocols do not apply to this Track. Many of the rules are relaxed in relation to the Small Claims Track and the procedure is designed to be used by those with no legal experience. The hearing is informal and there are strict limits on the costs that can be recovered (see below).

The **Fast Track** is most appropriate for claims that are worth up to £15,000, where the trial is likely to take only one day in court (five hours) and where only two separate fields of expertise are to be considered by the court. In deciding whether to allocate a case to the Fast Track, the court will take into account the expert evidence the parties are proposing to bring, the amount of documentary evidence that will be disclosed and relied upon and whether or not there is a counterclaim. Once allocated to the Fast Track, the court will issue 'directions' which deal with the bureaucratic steps leading to trial. The aim is to hold the trial not more than 30 weeks (about seven months) from the giving of directions. Some cases may be suitable for a 'case management conference' held at court or by telephone conference. This is a hearing at which the court will deal with administrative issues and give directions.

The **Multi Track** is the Track suitable for cases that are not suitable for allocation to the Small Claims or Fast Track. This will include cases that are 'worth' more that £15,000 and those that involve a great deal of expert evidence, complex legal argument, or where the trial is likely to take more than one day. The court will give directions, usually at a case management conference. Unlike Fast Track cases, however, the court will not set a trial date at this stage.

Directions for trial

The court has wide powers to make 'directions' for the preparation of the case for trial. It can make directions of its own initiative, or grant a direction sought by one of the parties. It is quite common that parties will be able to agree a timetable of steps. Unless very controversial or delaying, the court is usually happy to make the agreed order. This has the advantage that the timetable of directions will suit the needs of the parties from the outset and avoid the need of extensions of time which may imperil the readiness for trial.

Small Claims directions

Usually standard directions are made, although the court may in an unusual case make different directions. The parties may also ask for specific directions by filling in an Application Notice. The standard directions for a Small Claims Track case are as follows:

- Each party shall deliver to every other party and to the court office copies of all documents on which he intends to rely at the hearing no later than [date][14 days before the hearing].

- The original documents shall be brought to the hearing.

Highlight

The court has wide powers to make 'directions' for the preparation of the case for trial.

- The court may specify the details of the hearing, i.e. time date and duration.

- The court must be informed immediately if the case is settled by agreement before the hearing date.

The standard directions for claims arising from road accidents are as follows:

- Each party shall deliver to every other party and to the court office copies of all documents on which he intends to rely at the hearing. These may include **experts' reports** (including medical reports where damages for personal injuries are claimed), witness statements, invoices and estimates for repairs, and documents that relate to other losses, such as loss of earnings, sketch plans and photographs.

- The copies shall be delivered no later than [date][14 days before the hearing].

- The original documents should be brought to the hearing.

- Before the date of the hearing the parties shall try to agree the cost of the repairs and any other losses claimed, subject to the court's decision about whose fault the accident was.

- Signed statements setting out the evidence of all witnesses on whom each party intends to rely shall be prepared and copies included in the documents mentioned above.

- The parties should note that: (a) in deciding the case, the court will find it very helpful to have a sketch plan and photographs of the place where the accident happened; and (b) the court may decide not to take into account a document or the evidence of a witness if no copy of that document or no copy of a statement or report by that witness has been supplied to the other parties.

- Time, date and expected duration of the hearing.

- The court must be informed immediately if the case is settled by agreement before the hearing date.

Fast and Multi Track directions

The court will usually order the following: disclosure of documents, exchange of witness statements, exchange of experts' reports and the completion of 'listing questionnaires'. This means that each party must write a list of all the documents in his possession that relate to the case. The list should comprise documents that form part of his case (for example, his medical records or repair estimates), documents 'adverse' to another party's case and documents 'adverse' to his own case. The list of documents is sent to the other parties, who then may 'inspect' the documents listed (i.e. physically looking at the documents and making photocopies). It is becoming normal practice for a party to send photocopies of the documents mentioned in the list when the list is sent, which avoids the need of the receiving party formally to inspect them at the opponent's premises.

Witness statements

The general rule is that at trial, evidence is given orally. However, witness statements are crucial to the preparation of trial. A fundamental principle in English law is that each party should know what case the other party will be putting, so that he has time to prepare to deal with it. Witness statements are therefore exchanged before the trial so that all the parties may examine the evidence brought by the other side. Additionally, written evidence in the form of witness statements will (usually) be read by the judge prior to the trial, which saves court time. Finally, when a witness goes into the box to give his evidence he will usually only be asked to confirm the contents of the statement. With the permission of the court he may make any clarifying points (hopefully not necessary) and bring the court up to date on any events or developments since the statement was signed. Apart from this 'introductory and clarificatory' evidence, almost all of the oral evidence given by a witness will be his cross-examination evidence. The witness statement should therefore be as full as possible.

The witness statement should:

- identify the witness's name and address;

Highlight

A fundamental principle in English law is that each party should know what case the other party will be putting, so that he has time to prepare to deal with it.

- tell the witness's own story (identifying those parts which are his own direct knowledge and those parts which he knows from another source ('hearsay' – see below);

- be verified by a 'statement of truth';

- be signed and dated;

- 'exhibit' copies of documents mentioned in the witness statement in a separate document (see the sample front sheet below);

- give a page reference in the margin of the witness statement for any document mentioned;

- be in the following form: on A4 paper with a 3.5cm margin; typed only on one side of each page; bound together securely (i.e. by stapling the top left-hand corner – this does not interfere with filing), with numbered paragraphs, numbered pages and any corrections initialled.

Hearsay

Usually, one gives evidence of matters that one has experienced – for example, an eyewitness account of an accident. Sometimes, however, knowledge of a fact comes from a different source – an example might be an account of what one has read in a newspaper, or recounting what another person told one. This latter category is known as 'hearsay'. An example of hearsay evidence is given in the sample witness statement on page 106. The witness, Frank Whortley, gives evidence that he heard someone say, 'Oh, she's tripped over the carpet!' The fact that Frank heard someone speak the words is 'direct evidence' – he heard the words spoken. However, it is only hearsay evidence of the fact that Mrs Darling *actually* tripped over the carpet. Frank cannot *know* that she tripped over the carpet because he did not see her do so. He is passing on the eyewitness evidence of another person. The only people who can give 'direct evidence' of the fact that Mrs Darling tripped over the carpet are the customer and Mrs Darling herself. Frank's evidence is useful in that he can give direct evidence of the surrounding circumstances, particularly the position Mrs Darling was in after she had fallen.

Example witness statement

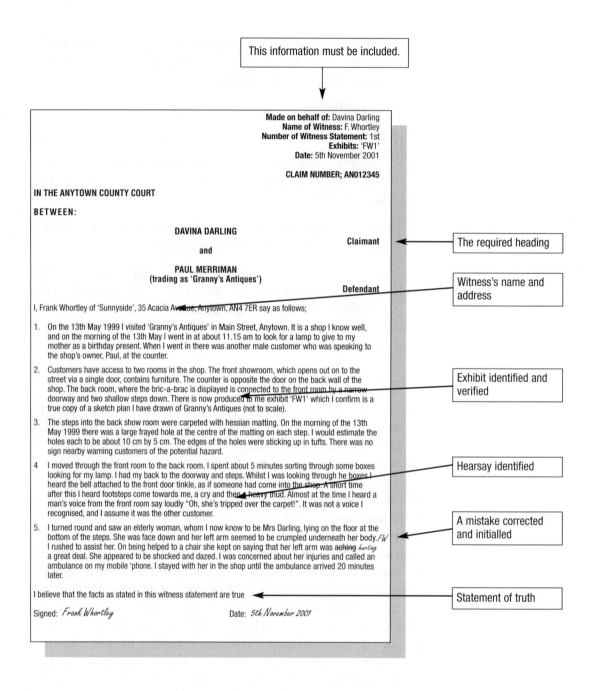

This information must be included.

Made on behalf of: Davina Darling
Name of Witness: F. Whortley
Number of Witness Statement: 1st
Exhibits: 'FW1'
Date: 5th November 2001

CLAIM NUMBER; AN012345

IN THE ANYTOWN COUNTY COURT

BETWEEN:

DAVINA DARLING

Claimant ← The required heading

and

PAUL MERRIMAN
(trading as 'Granny's Antiques')

Defendant ← Witness's name and address

I, Frank Whortley of 'Sunnyside', 35 Acacia Avenue, Anytown, AN4 7ER say as follows;

1. On the 13th May 1999 I visited 'Granny's Antiques' in Main Street, Anytown. It is a shop I know well, and on the morning of the 13th May I went in at about 11.15 am to look for a lamp to give to my mother as a birthday present. When I went in there was another male customer who was speaking to the shop's owner, Paul, at the counter.

2. Customers have access to two rooms in the shop. The front showroom, which opens out on to the street via a single door, contains furniture. The counter is opposite the door on the back wall of the shop. The back room, where the bric-a-brac is displayed is connected to the front room by a narrow doorway and two shallow steps down. There is now produced to me exhibit 'FW1' which I confirm is a true copy of a sketch plan I have drawn of Granny's Antiques (not to scale). ← Exhibit identified and verified

3. The steps into the back show room were carpeted with hessian matting. On the morning of the 13th May 1999 there was a large frayed hole at the centre of the matting on each step. I would estimate the holes each to be about 10 cm by 5 cm. The edges of the holes were sticking up in tufts. There was no sign nearby warning customers of the potential hazard.

4. I moved through the front room to the back room. I spent about 5 minutes sorting through some boxes looking for my lamp. I had my back to the doorway and steps. Whilst I was looking through the boxes I heard the bell attached to the front door tinkle, as if someone had come into the shop. A short time after this I heard footsteps come towards me, a cry and then a heavy thud. Almost at the time I heard a man's voice from the front room say loudly "Oh, she's tripped over the carpet!". It was not a voice I recognised, and I assume it was the other customer. ← Hearsay identified

5. I turned round and saw an elderly woman, whom I now know to be Mrs Darling, lying on the floor at the bottom of the steps. She was face down and her left arm seemed to be crumpled underneath her body. *FW* I rushed to assist her. On being helped to a chair she kept on saying that her left arm was ~~aching~~ *hurting* a great deal. She appeared to be shocked and dazed. I was concerned about her injuries and called an ambulance on my mobile 'phone. I stayed with her in the shop until the ambulance arrived 20 minutes later. ← A mistake corrected and initialled

I believe that the facts as stated in this witness statement are true ← Statement of truth

Signed: *Frank Whortley*   Date: *5th November 2001*

(Continued on next page)

Example witness statement (continued)

This information must be included.

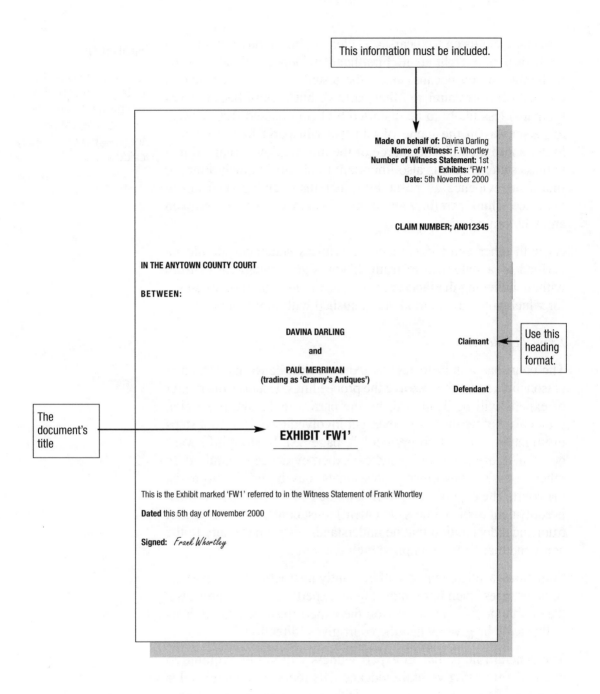

Made on behalf of: Davina Darling
Name of Witness: F. Whortley
Number of Witness Statement: 1st
Exhibits: 'FW1'
Date: 5th November 2000

CLAIM NUMBER; AN012345

IN THE ANYTOWN COUNTY COURT

BETWEEN:

DAVINA DARLING

and

**PAUL MERRIMAN
(trading as 'Granny's Antiques')**

Claimant

Use this heading format.

Defendant

The document's title

EXHIBIT 'FW1'

This is the Exhibit marked 'FW1' referred to in the Witness Statement of Frank Whortley

Dated this 5th day of November 2000

Signed: *Frank Whortley*

The court can listen to 'hearsay evidence', but it may not attach a great deal of weight to it. First-hand evidence will always be preferable, partly because it can be tested by cross-examination (and is therefore fairer to other parties), but mainly because it is (perhaps) less likely to be distorted by being passed from person to person (as in the game of Chinese whispers). It is therefore important to identify the source of the information contained in a witness statement. It is also important to obtain as much direct or first-hand evidence as possible, rather than relying on hearsay evidence. Think carefully about what evidence needs to be given and who can give it.

As with other court documents, a witness statement should be verified by a statement of truth. If you sign a statement of truth without believing the facts are true, you are in 'contempt of court' for which you may be tried and punished with imprisonment.

Expert evidence

The court has a duty to restrict expert evidence to that which is reasonably required to resolve the proceedings. Usually, the matter of experts will be dealt with by the parties under the pre-action protocols, before the courts ever get involved (see 'The first steps in litigation: 'pre-action protocols'', page 83). In straightforward personal injury cases, only medical expert evidence is required. In other cases, various other professionals may be needed to assist the court. The expert's duty is first to the court. The report (which is equivalent to his witness statement) must contain a statement of truth and a declaration that he understands his primary duty to the court and that he has complied with that duty.

Sometimes a single expert will be jointly instructed by the parties. In other cases, each party may call an expert witness. In any case, the court's permission to rely on the expert must be sought. This will usually be given when the court gives 'directions'.

The general rule is that an expert witness will not be required to attend the trial to give oral evidence. His report will stand as his evidence. Parties that wish to clarify a point made by another party's expert may ask him written questions about his report. This must be done within 28 days of receiving his report. The answers given are treated as part of the report. Sometimes the court will order two (or more) expert witnesses of the same field to conduct

Highlight

It is also important to obtain as much direct or first-hand evidence as possible, rather than relying on hearsay evidence.

an experts' meeting (by telephone or face to face) in order to draw up a 'statement of agreed facts' or 'statement of issues in dispute'. If an expert's report seems to be controversial or there is a dispute between the experts, it may be appropriate for the party wishing to cross-examine the other side's expert to ask the court to order that the expert attend the trial so as to give oral evidence.

Listing questionnaires

The court may send out 'listing questionnaires' and parties will have a certain time in which to complete them. As the name implies, a listing questionnaire is a form that enables the administrative staff at the court to allocate resources to the case. It describes how many witnesses will be called by a party, whether any special facilities will be needed by any of them (for example, an interpreter), how long the case is likely to last, the level of judge required, whether any further applications are likely to be made, etc.

Applications in the period before trial

There are many reasons why it will be necessary for a party to apply to the court for a particular order or permission. A party may want an extension of time to comply with a court order, or permission to rely on further evidence, or to vary directions made by the court. Where a party has failed to file a defence, the claimant may ask the court for a 'default' judgment. Similarly, where either the claimant or the defendant feels that the other party has no 'reasonable prospects of success' and there is no other reason why there should be a trial, he can apply to the court for a 'summary judgment'. All such applications are made on Form N244 (Application Notice), which should be sent to the court where the claim is being dealt with. Further copies of the form and the evidence referred to in the form should be served on the other parties in the case. Usually the court will consider whether or not it can deal with the application fairly without a hearing and if a hearing is necessary it will set a date and inform all the parties. The normal rule is that a 'respondent' to an application should have three clear days' notice of the application before the hearing date. On rare emergency occasions, a party may go before the court and make his application without telling the other party. This is known as an 'application without notice'. If an order is made,

Form N244 (Application Notice)

Application Notice

In the	

You should provide this information for listing the application

1. How do you wish to have your application dealt with

    a) at a hearing? ☐   *complete all questions below*

    b) at a telephone conference? ☐

    c) without a hearing? ☐   *complete Qs 5 and 6 below*

2. Give a time estimate for the hearing/conference
   _____ (hours)_____ (mins)

3. Is this agreed by all parties? ☐ Yes   ☐ No

4. Give dates of any trial period or fixed trial date _____

5. Level of judge _____

6. Parties to be served _____

Claim no.	
Warrant no. (if applicable)	
Claimant (including ref.)	
Defendant(s) (including ref.)	
Date	

Note You must complete Parts A **and** B, **and** Part C if applicable. Send any relevant fee and the completed application to the court with any draft order, witness statement or other evidence; and sufficient copies for service on each respondent.

Part A

1. Enter your full name, or name of solicitor   I (We)[1] _____ (on behalf of)(the claimant)(the defendant)

2. State clearly what order you are seeking and if possible attach a draft   intend to apply for an order (a draft of which is attached) that[2]

3. Briefly set out why you are seeking the order. Include the material facts on which you rely, identifying any rule or statutory provision   because[3]

Part B

I (We) wish to rely on: tick one box

     the attached (witness statement)(affidavit) ☐   my statement of case ☐

4. If you are not already a party to the proceedings, you must provide an address for service of documents   evidence in Part C in support of my application ☐

Signed		**Position or office held**	
(Applicant)('s Solicitor)('s litigation friend)		(if signing on behalf of firm or company)	

Address to which documents about this claim should be sent (including reference if appropriate)[4]

	if applicable	
	fax no.	
	DX no.	
Tel. no. Postcode	e-mail	

The court office at

is open from 10am to 4pm Monday to Friday. When corresponding with the court please address forms or letters to the Court Manager and quote the claim number.

N244 Application Notice (4.00)   *Reproduced by Law Pack Publishing with the permission of the Controller of HMSO*

Guidance notes provided

(Continued on next page)

Part C

Claim No.

I (We) wish to rely on the following evidence in support of this application:

Statement of Truth

*(I believe) *(The applicant believes) that the facts stated in Part C are true

*delete as appropriate

Signed

(Applicant)('s solicitor)('s litigation friend)

Position or
office held

(if signing on behalf
of firm or company)

Date

the court will set a new date for a hearing where the application can be fully argued by both sides.

The trial: what to expect

Preparing for the trial

Everyone, of course, will prepare for the trial in a way that they are comfortable. Just remember, you do not have to be Perry Mason; the aim should be to put your case simply and clearly to the judge. Notes, flow diagrams, checklists and sticky Post-it Notes may come in useful. A highlighter pen and a calculator may also be helpful.

CHECKLIST

After directions have been given:

❑ Have all the directions been complied with?

❑ Are there any necessary applications to the court?

❑ Can the amount of damages be agreed with the other side, subject to the judge deciding who is at fault? (This will avoid the need to prove the amount of your losses.)

Once a trial date has been given

❑ Have all directions been complied with?

❑ Have your witnesses been told the time and place of the trial?

❑ Have your witnesses confirmed they will attend?

Preparing for the hearing

❑ Are there any applications that need to be made?

❑ List the issues in dispute: has quantum or liability been agreed? What parts of each witness's evidence are controversial. What parts are not disputed? It will save everyone time and money if you can tell the judge what areas of agreement and disagreement remain. This will enable the judge to focus on the areas he must adjudicate upon.

Highlight

Just remember, you do not have to be Perry Mason; the aim should be to put your case simply and clearly to the judge.

❑ Have you prepared the questions you wish to ask in cross-examination?

❑ What extra information (by way of clarification or updating) should the witnesses give to the court to supplement their witness statements?

❑ Are you ready to summarise the facts of the case for the judge?

On the day of the trial

❑ Arrive at court in plenty of time and report in to the usher.

❑ Read through your witness statement.

❑ Meet your witnesses (do not discuss their evidence with them, but give them a copy of their statements to read so that they can confirm the contents to the court).

❑ Are there any last-minute applications that need to be made to the judge? If so, let the other parties know what you are asking for.

During the trial

❑ It may be helpful to take a note of the evidence given by the witnesses, as well as the judgment delivered at the end.

❑ Jot down any weakness in the other side's case, when you spot it, so you can draw the judge's attention to it when you summarise your case.

❑ Although the court will send out a copy of the order made at the end of the trial, this may take some weeks to be sent to you so it is wise to make a note of the judge's order (if necessary ask him to read it out aloud at the end).

Arriving at court

Make sure you arrive early enough for the hearing or trial. This will give you time to gather your thoughts and prepare yourself for the hearing. It will also give you an opportunity to speak to the other side before going in front of the judge. It may be possible to do a deal on the doorstep of the court. Alternatively, it may be an opportunity to discuss with the other party (especially if they are represented by a lawyer) exactly what issues you agree and disagree about. The more agreement there is and the more pleasant co-operation between parties, the easier the hearing will be. Of course, this is a matter of personality (your own as well as your opponent's), but you might as well give yourself the opportunity of learning what stance your opponent is taking before the hearing.

Always leave plenty of time for a court hearing. Often a case that is 'listed' for a morning hearing will end up being heard after lunch. This will involve you making appropriate contingency plans (parking, time off work, child care arrangements, etc.). On rare occasions, the judge may feel there is not enough time to hear the case and will 'adjourn' it to another date. The usher will keep you informed.

The most important person in the whole legal system is the court usher. On arriving at court you must 'report in' to the usher dealing with your particular court. You will first need to identify where your case will be heard. Many courts have a security guard at the door with a list of cases to be heard in each court who will direct parties to the correct courtroom. Otherwise, there will be a 'cause list' near the entrance, with lists of where cases will be heard.

The usher will introduce you to your opponents when they arrive and if you need any extra negotiation time, ask the usher to have a word with the judge. Do not leave the building without telling the usher; your case could be called on whilst you are away. Finally, the usher will be able to tell you where to stand in court.

Where to stand and what to wear

There are no rules of court dress for litigants-in-person. Lawyers and judges will wear dark suits and in open court will usually be robed and be wearing wigs. A typical courtroom layout is provided on page 115.

The trial

Small Claims Track hearings

The hearing will usually take place in the district judge's office (known as 'chambers'). Technically, the hearing takes place in public and anyone may come and watch. Usually, only friends and

Typical courtroom layout

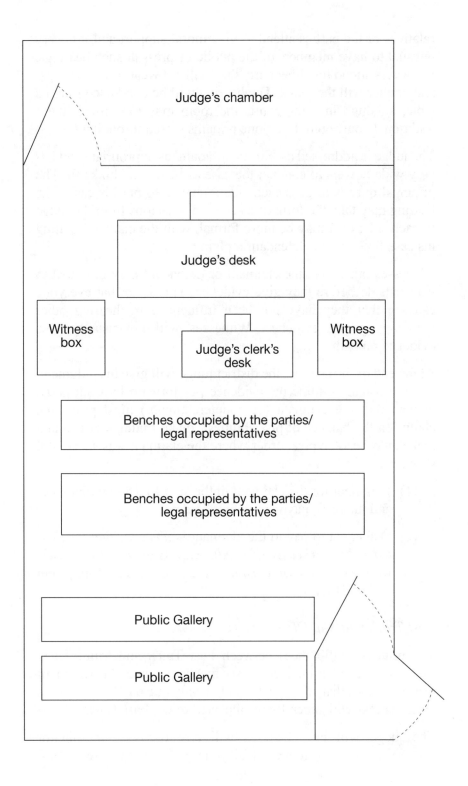

relatives of the parties attend to give moral support and it is very unusual to have members of the public or press at such hearings. If lawyers attend for either party they will not wear robes (or wigs) and neither will the judge. The hearing will be conducted round a table, although in some courts the room may look more like a traditional courtroom. Everyone remains seated throughout.

The judge is addressed as 'Sir' or 'Madam' as appropriate and has very wide powers to conduct the case as he or she thinks fit. The principal duty is to give each side a chance to put his case. The hearing may take the form of a series of questions from the judge to each side; or it may be more formal, with the claimant putting his case first and the defendant replying.

Witnesses other than the claimant or defendant may be asked to wait outside before they give evidence. This is so that everyone can see that they have not been influenced by hearing other witnesses giving evidence. Witnesses will not usually give evidence on oath.

At the end of the hearing, the district judge will give his judgment. He will usually outline the evidence put forward by each party, explain that the claimant (or counterclaimant) must prove the claim 'on the balance of probabilities', make findings of fact and make an order. A typical order where the claimant was successful may read:

(1) Judgment for the claimant in the sum £1,188.99 (damages and interest); payment within 21 days.

(2) Defendant to pay to the claimant [*sums specified for limited solicitors' costs (if used), witnesses' travel expenses, witnesses' loss of earnings (limited to £50)*] payment within 21 days.

Fast Track and Multi Track trials

The principal differences between Fast Track and Multi Track trials are the rules on legal costs that apply and the length of hearing. Cases that are expected to last only one day (five hours in court) or less will generally be allocated to the Fast Track.

The judge will be robed, as will any barrister or solicitor appearing. 'Circuit judges' (full-time judges) and 'recorders' (experienced barristers/solicitors who act as judges for a certain period each year) are addressed as 'Your Honour'. District judges are addressed as 'Sir' or 'Madam'. Justice must be seen to be done and the trial will be conducted in public, which means that anyone may enter the courtroom during the hearing and there are no reporting restrictions. However, the judge may order the hearing to be in private in special circumstances.

After dealing with any applications or 'housekeeping matters' to do with the conduct of the trial, the judge will let the parties know how familiar he is with the papers. All judges are different. Some like to prepare meticulously in advance; many will not have had a chance to look at the papers beforehand (for example, where the case has only just been assigned to his court). The judge may state clearly how he wants to run the case at the outset.

The running order of a normal trial is as follows:

- Claimant 'opens the case', briefly explaining the case for the judge.

- Claimant 'calls his evidence'.

- Defendant 'calls his evidence'.

- Defendant makes his 'closing speech'.

- Claimant makes his 'closing speech'.

- Judge gives his 'judgment' there and then and makes the 'order' OR judge 'reserves judgment' to be given with the appropriate order later.

THE CLAIMANT'S OPENING SPEECH

Judges may not require the claimant to make an opening speech, especially if the dispute is straightforward. What follows, therefore, is a somewhat artificial example. However, it is better to be prepared and not to have to use it than the other way around!

1. An opening speech should give the judge an overview of the type of case:

    'Your Honour will see from the papers that this is my claim for personal injuries arising from a road traffic accident/ an accident at work, etc.'

Highlight

All judges are different. Some like to prepare meticulously in advance; many will not have had a chance to look at the papers beforehand.

2. It also helps to tell the judge what facts are agreed between the parties:

'We both agree that the accident happened on the 3rd January 2001, at the junction of Easterhall Lane and Marketcross Avenue. There is no dispute that the accident happened in the dark and that it had just been raining. On that night I was a pedestrian, and the defendant was driving a Ford Fiesta, registration QWE 45T. Your Honour, only 'liability' is in dispute. Special damages have been agreed in the sum of £856.23, and the medical evidence has been agreed.'

3. ...and what is disputed:

'My case is that the defendant drove negligently, and knocked me over as I crossed the road; the defendant denies it, and says that she could not avoid the accident; she claims I ran out in front of her.'

4. Lastly, give an overview of the evidence that will be called by both sides:

'I will give evidence, as will my sister who was waiting for me on the other side of the road. Mr Smith, an independent witness who saw the accident from a parked car at the junction, will give evidence on my behalf. The defendant is giving evidence for himself, and will also call PC Constable who was called to the scene. The jointly instructed expert is not in court today, but his report is on page 5 of the bundle of papers in front of Your Honour.'

It may also be useful to refer the judge at this point to any documents (such as invoices, receipts, employment records, contracts, etc.) relied upon by either party. Often there will be photographs or maps and the judge should be shown these, told who relies upon them, and whether they are 'agreed'.

The judge SHOULD NOT be told about or shown any 'without prejudice' discussions or letters. He does not find out about any 'payments into court' (see 'Payments into court and 'Part 36 offers'', page 127) or attempts to settle the case.

Highlight

The Judge SHOULD NOT be told about or shown any 'without prejudice' discussions or letters.

THE EVIDENCE

Witnesses will give evidence on oath (or 'affirmation', for those who prefer a secular promise) and stand in the witness box. Having been asked to confirm their name and address and to verify their signature and the contents of the witness statement, the witness evidence will stand as their actual evidence. The judge may, if he has not had the opportunity to read it, do so at this point in silence, or ask the witness (or advocate) to read it aloud. Some witnesses may need to bring their statements up to date if there have been any developments or changes since they were made.

After a witness gives his evidence, the other party may 'cross-examine' him. This is not an easy technique and advocates have many different styles and approaches. There are two main purposes of cross-examination:

- to challenge the other side's witness with the evidence that you rely on;

- to expose any contradictions, gaps or weaknesses in the other side's case.

Often minute discrepancies in observation or recall may make all the difference; witnesses may be unsure of certain parts of their evidence, or may have made assumptions about what happened that are not born out by other evidence.

CLOSING ARGUMENTS

This is an opportunity for both claimant and defendant to summarise the strengths of their own case and to highlight the weaknesses of the other side's. Any 'submissions' on how the law applies to the case will be made at this stage, e.g. references to relevant Acts of Parliament, regulations, other codes (such as the Highway Code) and case law. Finally, tell the judge what order you are asking him to make (dismiss the claim/defence/counter-claim, award damages, etc.)

Costs

The section 'How do I fund my claim or defence' on page 70 discusses how to pay for legal costs from the beginning of the claim. This section sets out the rules used by the court to order one side to pay the other side's costs at the end of the trial.

After giving judgment, the judge will decide if either party should pay the legal costs of the other side. If the court makes no such order each party simply 'bears his own' costs. Usually the 'loser' will be told to pay the other side's costs (legal and experts' fees, court fees and other expenses). The loser will probably have to pay:

- his own legal bill;

- the legal bill of the other side (after it has been 'assessed' by the court);

- damages.

Of course, as with all costs, a party can only obtain an award for costs that he has incurred, or will incur under a 'conditional fee agreement'. Therefore, proof of costs by way of receipts, a 'schedule of costs' or 'bill of costs' may be required by the court.

Small Claims costs

The Small Claims Track is designed for litigants who are not represented by a lawyer. As a result, neither party is expected to run up large legal bills and therefore a party may only recover very limited legal costs under CPR Part 27:

Legal costs

- the 'fixed costs' of issuing the claim (between £50 and £80 at present, depending on the size of the claim) if he has used a lawyer to issue the claim;

- other legal costs where the judge has decided that the other side has behaved 'unreasonably' in the conduct of the case.

Fees and expenses

- court fees;

- a witness's or party's travel expenses (reasonably incurred) for attendance at the hearing;

- a witness's or party's loss of earnings incurred through attendance at the hearing (limited to £50 each at present);

- the fees of any expert witness (limited to £200 each at present).

Fast Track and Multi Track costs

The general rules for determining costs apply to both Fast Track and Multi Track cases. The court has a discretion whether to award costs, how much to order a party to pay and when the payment should be made. The recoverable fees of advocates (barristers or solicitors) and solicitors attending Fast Track trials are fixed within certain limits, but of course this is only one element of a costs bill. The amount recoverable in respect of advocate's fee for appearing at trial depends on the amount of the claim:

- claim value is up to £3,000   £350

- £3,000–£10,000   £500

- more than £10,000   £750

The court may in certain circumstances award less than the fixed amount (i.e. where there has been a successful counterclaim, where the receiving party has behaved improperly during the trial). The court may order the paying party to pay more than the fixed amounts where he has acted improperly or unreasonably during the trial.

Where the party being awarded his costs by the court acted in person, the court may award him two-thirds of the appropriate fee had an advocate attended the trial (as above), if he proves financial loss arising from conducting his own claim. If he cannot prove financial loss, the court will award an amount in respect of the time reasonably spent doing the work, at certain specified rates.

In all Multi Track cases and Fast Track cases where the litigant-in-person who is asking for a costs order is not able to prove financial loss in personally conducting the claim, the rules stipulate that the litigant-in-person can be paid:

(i) his expenses or disbursements, including travel expenses to court;

(ii) recompense for financial loss in preparing the case and attending court (for which supporting documentary evidence should be served 24 hours before the hearing at which costs will be delivered) **or** £9.25 per hour (current rate), **but** the sum allowed for this particular type of loss will only be two-thirds of the sum that he would be allowed if he had been represented by a legal representative;

(iii) the cost of obtaining legal services (if incurred reasonably) from a solicitor or barrister, or a 'costs draftsman'.

In short, the court will first consider if the other party should pay your costs. It will then consider the evidence of financial loss (for example, your loss of earnings) during the time you prepared for the case, or attended court hearings. If there is no evidence of financial loss it will decide that you will be paid at an hourly rate, currently £9.25. The judge will decide if the period you spent in preparing the case and attending court was reasonable, and state what period he does think would have been reasonable. He will then decide what sum would have been payable if you had instructed solicitors and will not award more than two-thirds of that sum. Finally the judge will look at all the expenses and disbursements you have incurred and award those.The court must decide whether or not it can assess the costs at the end of a trial (immediately after judgment is given), or whether the complexity of the case and the amount of costs incurred merits a separate hearing in front of a specialist 'costs judge' called a 'detailed assessment' of costs.

A litigant cannot be ordered to pay any costs that are 'unreasonable' in amount or which have been unreasonably incurred. Usually only costs which are 'proportionate' to the dispute will be awarded. Generally, therefore, the paying party will not be ordered to pay the full amount of the other side's costs. Put the other way around, a successful party rarely recoups all his legal costs.

Costs may be also used as a sanction or 'punishment' against a party, for example, if earlier orders of the court are not complied with. On rare occasions a lawyer who has acted unconscionably or negligently may be ordered to pay any 'wasted costs' personally. On the Small Claims Track mere 'unreasonable conduct' may result in a cost order (see above). Failure to comply with a pre-action protocol may also lead to a higher costs award against a party.

Settling 'out of court'

When can a claim be settled?

A potential claim between parties may be settled at various stages:

- in a contract before court proceedings are begun;

- in a 'compromise' or 'settlement' after proceedings have started, at any time before the judge has given judgment (thus a settlement may be reached even after the judge has heard all the evidence and closing speeches!).

The pre-action protocols are designed to promote early settlement and judges will often assist parties by giving them time to negotiate, if it looks as though there are real prospects of a deal being struck.

The advantages of settlement

Whilst the new rules of court are designed to promote co-operation between the parties (and to stop tactical games), the English and Welsh system is still an 'adversarial' one. The judge does not investigate facts in an attempt to uncover the truth; instead the parties present the evidence supporting their version of events for him to decide which he prefers. A great deal will depend on the witness evidence 'on the day'. A key witness may not attend (although it is possible to compel attendance by issuing a 'witness summons'); a witness may fall apart under cross-examination, or simply be disbelieved. It may be just that the other side's evidence is stronger, clearer or more credible. Litigation is therefore unpredictable, expensive and stressful.

A case may take considerable time to go through the courts. The trial may occur some years after the accident. Even Fast Track cases, which are intended to have a timetable of 30 weeks (about seven months) between directions and trial, are not particularly 'fast'. The initial stages of obtaining medical reports and complying with the pre-action protocols may take considerable time. Then there are the preparations for trial, described above. Lastly, there is the matter of 'listing' the case for trial. A court may be very busy, and trial dates may be fixed far ahead, particularly if the case is to last more than one day in court. Settlement of a case prevents further costs being incurred. If money is involved the payer need not incur any interest (calculated perhaps from the date of the accident) on damages, and the payee receives his money earlier than he would otherwise do so.

How and when to negotiate

Settlement involves negotiation. Inevitably, personal injury claims will be about money compensation. Just as a claim (or counter-claim) has a value, so do the risks of litigation. Those risks must be assessed at every stage, especially as they may change as the case develops. A weak claim or defence has less value than a strong one. The weaker party has less to bargain with and therefore may have to settle for less. The purpose of negotiation is to find the 'magic sum'; in an ideal world this will be the highest a claimant can obtain and the least the defendant will pay.

Negotiations are not drawn to the court's attention until a deal is struck. Therefore all letters, faxes and e-mails that genuinely aim to negotiate towards settlement are 'without prejudice' and are usually clearly marked with this phrase. Similarly, without prejudice negotiations may be conducted orally over the telephone or face to face. It should be made clear that all negotiations are just that and that discussions are 'without prejudice' to the party's case. If negotiations break down the parties move towards trial in the normal way.

Negotiation is a matter of personality, style and confidence. Some people (lawyers included!) are conciliatory in their approach; others are bullish. Keep the following things clearly in mind before entering negotiations:

- the 'value' of the claim – even if you are the defendant (see chapter 5);

- the strength and weaknesses of your own case;

- the strength and weaknesses of the other party's case.

The terms of the settlement

Remember, the settlement will bring all the matters between the parties to an end. It must tie up all loose ends, as generally it is not

---

Highlight

The purpose of negotiation is to find the 'magic sum'; in an ideal world this will be the highest a claimant can obtain and the least the defendant will pay.

Example consent order

IN THE BLANKTOWN COUNTY COURT
B E T W E E N

Harinda Singh

Claimant

and

John Brown

Defendant

ON this 13th day of December 2000
BEFORE His Honour Judge Lockhart
BY CONSENT IT IS ORDERED:

(1)   The Defendant to pay the Claimant £15,500 by the 7th March 2001

(2)   [There be no order as to costs] [the Defendant to pay the Claimant's costs assessed at £4,501.02 by 7th March 2001] [the Defendant to pay the Claimant's costs to be subject to detailed assessment if not agreed between the parties].

possible to go back to court with fresh issues, further complaints or new calculations.

The two main types of settlement are:

(a) the payment of money by the defendant to the claimant (or by the claimant to the defendant where there is a counter-claim); and

(b) a 'walk away deal' where no money is paid and each party agrees to end the litigation, each giving up his right to pursue his claim or defence.

A settlement may contain the following terms:

- the amount of damages and interest to be paid, by whom, to whom;

- the date of payment of the whole amount (or the dates of instalments);

- the amount of costs to be paid by a party (unless each side is to bear his own).

The form of a settlement

1. Before court proceedings:

   One party makes an offer that is accepted by the other. It is advisable for the terms agreed to be contained or confirmed in writing and it is important to make it clear that the contract is in 'full and final settlement' of matters arising from the accident. Once agreed, the contract is a defence to any future claim between the parties arising from the accident. If a party fails to comply with the terms the other party may bring a fresh claim (within six years) for breach of the contract.

2. After court proceedings have begun:

   The parties may come to an agreement at any time before the judge gives his judgment. A looming trial date concentrates minds wonderfully! It is advisable for the parties to put their agreement before the judge and ask him to make a 'consent order' (see example on page 125). Where a child (anyone under the age of 18) or 'patient' (someone who has a mental disorder within the meaning of the Mental Health Act 1983 and is incapable of managing his own affairs) is involved in the case, any settlement is not valid unless it has been 'approved' by the court.

Payments into court and 'Part 36 offers'

The defendant may make a payment of money into court in respect of settling all or part of the claim at any time after the claim is issued. The court looks after the money and then pays it:

a) to the claimant, upon the judge making an award of damages in his favour; or

b) to the claimant, upon his formally accepting the sum; otherwise

c) to the defendant.

The defendant must use Form N242A and the claimant will be informed of the payment. The claimant then has 21 days in which to accept or reject it. The offer cannot be withdrawn by the defendant unless the court gives permission. However, the defendant can increase the offer by paying more into court. The advantage to the defendant of offering to settle the action in this way is that if the claimant refuses the offer and then does not succeed at trial or is not awarded damages in a larger sum than that paid into court, the claimant must bear the defendant's legal costs from the last date of possible acceptance of the payment. For the defendant who wishes to settle his case, therefore, the procedure gives him some protection for his costs and thus is a useful tool with which to pressurise the claimant.

Conversely, a similar mechanism exists for the benefit of the claimant in the form of a 'Part 36 offer'. This is where the claimant makes an offer in writing to the defendant, usually that he will accept a specified sum of money to settle the case. The offer must remain open for 21 days. The consequences of the defendant rejecting the offer and then being found liable by the court for a greater sum are that the defendant will probably have to pay a considerable costs and interest bill.

The existence of rejected Part 36 payments and offers is not communicated to the trial judge until he has ruled on liability and quantum and is considering costs. If the Part 36 offer or payment is made less than 21 days before trial, the permission of the court is needed in order to accept the payment or offer (unless the parties agree between them who shall pay the legal costs). Note also that the cost consequences of Part 36 payments and offers do not apply to Small Claim Track cases.

How compensation is calculated

5

The law in England and Wales attempts to compensate an injured person for the loss he has suffered, rather than punish the person responsible for the injuries. Once liability has been decided, therefore, the court turns to the claimant to 'prove' his loss. Loss is usually divided into 'direct loss' (such as injury, damage to vehicles, clothes, etc.) and 'consequential loss' arising from the direct loss (such as lost earnings, medical and care expenses, etc.). Thus a claimant's claim for damages will comprise:

- 'Special damages': all the expenses and other losses quantifiable in monetary terms incurred between the accident and trial (such as damaged clothing, vehicle repairs or value and loss of earnings). Special damages must be listed in a 'schedule of special damages' which is attached to the Particulars of Claim (see 'Claimant: issuing a claim', page 89).

- 'General damages': damages for pain and suffering (past and future) arising from the injury, and anticipated future costs and losses (such as future medical expenses or equipment, future loss of earnings or 'handicap on the labour market').

The courts will generally only consider the case once and for all; the award of damages must encompass any future losses, pain and suffering or loss of amenity. In certain circumstances, the court will consider making an award for the time being, revisiting the claim at a later date – see 'Provisional damages awards', page 139.

Highlight

The courts will generally only consider the case once and for all; the award of damages must encompass any future losses, pain and suffering or loss of amenity.

Special damages are generally mere exercises in proof and calculation (see page 134, 'Compensation for financial loss and expenses up to the date of trial or settlement' and page 135, 'DSS benefits and the Compensation Recovery Unit 'clawback''). General damages are not so obviously quantifiable. The courts have had to devise a system which translates pain and suffering from an injury into a sum of damages. Similarly, the court has devised methods of calculating future losses to take account of the advantages of being awarded a lump-sum in advance of the likely time of loss (this is sometimes called 'accelerated receipt').

Compensation for 'pain, suffering and loss of amenity'

As the phrase suggests, this element of the award compensates for the pain and other suffering occasioned by an injury. The area is governed by case law and other guidelines such as the Judicial Studies Board Guidelines. These have resulted in a loose 'tariff' system, so that both claimants and defendants (and the insurance industry) can calculate the likely amount of an award from the outset. In other words, every injury has its 'value' in terms of damages. The law will take into account the following elements:

- the pain suffered;

- the recovery rate and prognosis;

- whether the symptoms are permanent;

- the extent of the treatment required (past and future);

- whether the symptoms have accelerated the onset of any other condition;

- whether the injuries have reduced life expectancy;

- the effect of the injury on the practicalities and enjoyment of everyday life, including damage to relationships, loss of job satisfaction, the ability to work and to look after oneself; to resume normal duties and responsibilities, and the pursuit of hobbies and interests;

Highlight

Every injury has its 'value' in terms of damages.

- the degree of shock, embarrassment, anxiety and any other emotional effects of the injury (though no claim can be made for this element alone);

- the age of the claimant.

The starting place is the Judicial Studies Board Guidelines. These class symptoms into general categories covering psychiatric conditions, paralysis, orthopaedic injuries, injuries to internal organs, injuries affecting the senses, scarring, facial injuries and brain damage. Within these categories, broad bands of likely awards reflect the severity or otherwise of the symptoms.

The Judicial Studies Board Guidelines are reproduced in the various textbooks used by lawyers. These resources also contain hundreds of case reports and the damages awarded (usually called 'quantum of general damages for personal injury'). You may find one of these textbooks in a library: *Kemp & Kemp, Current Law* and Butterworth's *Personal Injury Litigation Service.*

Lawyers calculate 'general damages' awards by taking the following steps. It is not a precise art, but the more research one does and the more comparable cases one finds, the easier it is to pinpoint the appropriate award:

- identify the guideline range from the Judicial Studies Board Guidelines;

- research case law to ascertain how the courts deal with cases of the same nature to the present one, trying to identify a reported case that is as near as possible on the facts;

- account for inflation (see below).

Because inflation renders the damages awarded and the Judicial Studies Board Guidelines out of date within a short period of time, lawyers update the likely award by using the following formula:

$$\frac{\text{Today's RPI} \times £\,[\text{expected award}]}{\text{RPI at the time of the award}}$$

The monthly Retail Price Index (RPI) is reported in *Current Law*, and in tables set out in *Kemp & Kemp* and Butterworths' *Personal Injury Litigation Service.* A Citizens Advice Bureau or library may be able to help you obtain any of these publications or the Retail Price Index.

Example

An award of £5,000 was made in March 1993 when the RPI was 139.30. The value of the award in December 2000 when the RPI was 171.7 is calculated as follows:

$$(171.7 \times £5,000) \div 139.3 = £6,162.95$$

Thus, at the date of calculation, December 2000, the award would be the equivalent of £6,162 and the court would take that into account when deciding the actual amount.

Where a person suffers more than one injury, the court is anxious to avoid 'double recovery'. This simply means that compensation for different elements is not merely added up, but there is some overlapping of compensation. Thus, in crude terms, the court will not add up, say, £1,000 for a whiplash injury, £450 for a hand injury, and £300 for a head injury and award £1,750. It will take into account that the pain and suffering comes largely from multiple injuries and where appropriate will consider the pain, suffering and loss of amenity together. In this example, therefore, and all other things being equal, the court would award a sum less than £1,750.

Case study

Joan Brown's stationary motorbike was hit from behind by a car. She was knocked to the ground and an ambulance was called. At Accident and Emergency she was found to have sustained a 3cm cut to her face, a soft tissue injury to her neck, bruising to both knees and upper legs. Her wound was cleaned and 'glued', she was given analgesics and a surgical collar and discharged. Joan, who is 34 years old, stayed in bed for one week and could not go to work. Her birthday party had to be cancelled and she was unable to resume her hobby of windsurfing for six months. When the specialist examined her, he agreed with the diagnosis and noted that her facial cut had healed after five weeks with a faint but permanent scar and the bruising on her legs had settled after two weeks. Her neck was very stiff and painful for two weeks after the accident and thereafter began to improve. Joan still suffered some residual symptoms when examined by the specialist six months after the accident. The specialist believed that the symptoms would settle completely in a further three months (nine months after the accident).

The award will take into account:

- *Joan has suffered multiple minor injuries and the court will not look at each injury separately, but rather consider them together.*

- *Joan suffered pain and discomfort for the first two weeks from her neck injury, the bruising and the cut; she was in bed for one week.*

- *After two weeks, her symptoms began to settle, with her bruising improving first, then the cut healed and finally her neck symptoms resolved. This occurred within the nine months after the accident.*

- *She missed one week of work, could not windsurf for six months and was disappointed to miss her birthday party.*

- *Joan's everyday life and her ability to care for herself were not affected beyond the first two weeks, when her mother came to look after her.*

- *She is a young woman, and in the specialist's view the injuries she sustained will have no long-term implications for her.*

Previous injury or a further accident before trial

Highlight

Where a claimant had a pre-existing condition, the court will only grant compensation to the extent to which the claimant was *further* injured, suffered loss, etc.

A defendant is only liable for the damage and injury he has caused. Where a claimant had a pre-existing condition, the court will only grant compensation to the extent to which the claimant was *further* injured, suffered loss, etc. Similarly, where before the trial or settlement the claimant suffers a separate incident, accident or disease, the court must avoid making the defendant compensate for the aggravation or exacerbation of any symptoms, or the increase of any loss caused by the second event. This is a matter in which medical evidence is particularly helpful.

Compensation for financial loss and expenses up to the date of trial or settlement

This element of a damages claim is known as 'special damages'; it is calculated arithmetically. Financial loss and other expenses that are caused by the accident itself, or are incurred because of the injuries, are recoverable. The claimant must 'prove his loss' by satisfying the court that he has incurred each expense or suffered each item of loss as a result of the accident. He must also quantify each item claimed by providing receipts and estimates. The court expects him also to 'mitigate his loss' (see 'The duty of the claimant to mitigate his loss', page 138). A failure to mitigate a particular loss may result in only partial recovery of the amount claimed.

English law requires the claimant to set out everything he is claiming at the outset. A 'schedule of special damages' is a pre-action stage required by the personal injury pre-action protocol (see page 85). This sets out each item of loss or expense and the amount claimed. Of course, as the matter progresses it will be necessary to update the schedule from time to time.

The items that can be claimed include:

- Cost of repairing property damaged in the accident (for example, clothing, spectacles, car, motorcycle or bicycle) or, if uneconomic, the value of the item prior to the accident.

- Cost of treatment (including private health care, prescription charges and travel expenses to hospital).

- The costs of 'disability' (including nursing charges and other reasonable paid help, the cost of necessary equipment such as crutches or specially adapted car and the increased costs of normal expenditure attributable to the injuries such as transport, home heating, etc.).

- The value of the unpaid care provided by a member of the family or friend to the claimant and the costs incurred by such carers visiting hospital, or taking unpaid time off work.

Highlight

A failure to mitigate a particular loss may result in only partial recovery of the amount claimed.

- Loss of earnings (net of contractual sick pay) or loss of earnings disregarding statutory sick pay (the value of the latter will be deducted by the defendant and paid to the government under the recovery of benefits scheme – see 'DSS benefits and the Compensation Recovery Unit 'clawback'', below), and the value of other employment benefits.

For a sample schedule of special damages, see 'Claimant: issuing a claim', page 89.

DSS benefits and the Compensation Recovery Unit 'clawback'

Under the Social Security (Recovery of Benefits) Act 1997, a defendant is obliged to repay the government for any Social Security benefits paid to the claimant as a result of the injury or disease for up to five years from the accident or, in the case of disease, from the date of the first benefit claim in respect of it. The defendant must apply to the DSS for a certificate of recoverable benefits (known as a CRU Certificate), and this will tell him how much benefit must be repaid to the government.

The classes of recoverable benefits are listed at Appendix 6. They fall broadly into three categories: loss of earnings, costs of care and loss of mobility. Where the claimant is claiming for a type of loss, such as loss of earnings, the defendant will deduct the amount of any recoverable benefits paid during that time relating to loss of earnings. The deduction can only be made from that particular element of his claim; it cannot be deducted from another 'head' of damage such as the element for pain and suffering. Nor can the deduction result in less than a payment to the claimant of nil, i.e. the claimant will not end up owing the defendant for deductions made by the defendant.

Compensation for future losses and expenses

These are often known as 'general damages for future loss'. The calculations are as from the date of trial or settlement. The aim is to compensate the claimant for any future losses arising from the accident (although not for future pain and discomfort of any disability which is contemplated in the general damages for pain and suffering component – see above). There is no magic formula that will apply to all cases; the court will need to take into account various contingencies and tailor the different arithmetical or statistical tools to provide the most accurate level of compensation. For example, the chances of future promotion, early retirement, or the statistical probability of a woman taking time out of employment to have children will all be relevant and will reflect not only the amount of damages, but also the way they are calculated.

Some types of damage will be a single item of expenditure; others will be a repeated loss or expense. In some cases, the claimant might only have needs for a few years; in others the disability or condition may be permanent, in which case life expectancy or retirement age may be part of the calculation.

The list below is not exhaustive but damages may include the following, where appropriate:

- future loss of earnings and/or for loss of earning capacity (also know as 'handicap on the labour market', where the claimant cannot expect to earn as much because of the accident);

- future costs of nursing care or other professional help (housekeeping, maintenance of the home);

- future costs of medication, treatment or equipment;

- the cost of adapting a home/car to meet the claimant's particular needs;

- the higher costs of living occasioned by the claimant's continuing condition;

- loss of future pension rights because of inability to maintain the pre-accident expected contributions.

The claimant must prove the likelihood of him suffering continuing or future losses and the reasonableness of the sums involved. He will need to produce estimates and other documentary proof of future costs. Medical evidence of a relevant specialist will be needed to prove evidence of the claimant's future care and treatment needs and also evidence of his future ability to work. Similarly, where the claimant claims future loss of earnings (because he cannot work at all, or his working life has been curtailed by the injuries) or handicap on the labour market, a forensic employment specialist will need to give evidence on his behalf.

Once a figure is obtained for each type of loss, the parties will need to establish if this is a 'once-only' expense, or if it is regularly recurring. An example of a once-only expense might be the increased cost of purchasing and adapting a bungalow, a figure that is easily obtainable.

Those items (such as specially adapted vehicles or equipment) that will only be incurred from time to time are, similarly, easy to calculate. An example might be the purchase of a wheelchair at £1,000 and its replacement every five years. Where the claimant can be expected to need a wheelchair for the rest of his life (he is 46 and has a life expectancy of 75, say) the future costs of wheelchairs for him will be: £1,000 × 5 (the number of times he will have to replace the wheelchair in his lifetime). Generally, the payment of a lump-sum for such expenses will obviate the need to take into account inflation and other future price rises.

Other ongoing losses can be calculated on an annual basis (except for loss of earning capacity – see below). This is a complex area and it is recommended that readers who are claiming or defending a case with significant periods of lost future earnings, or reduced life expectancy, take legal advice. This guide can only give an indication of the court's approach.

Once an annual figure of loss and expense is calculated, it must be multiplied by a suitable amount known as the 'multiplicand', to reflect the future period of continuing loss. The starting point is to consider the actual number of years the claimant is expecting to suffer this loss; is it for a short period or is it permanent? Lawyers use a series of actuarial tables called the Ogden Tables (now in their fourth edition), to find the appropriate multiplicand.

Loss of earning capacity

This phrase covers various types of damage to the future prospects of earning an income. It includes situations where the injuries have handicapped the claimant on the labour market, damaged his prospects of promotion, increased the likelihood of the claimant having to retire early or obtain lower-paid work. Quantifying such losses is not easy and often the starting point is one or two years' net pay.

The duty of the claimant to mitigate his loss

The claimant has a positive duty to take reasonable steps to minimise the damage he has suffered. The court will take account of the claimant's circumstances in deciding what is reasonable; failure to take the reasonable steps may result in a proportion of the damages suffered not being recovered.

Interest on damages

The court has the power to award interest on damages claims. This is a notional compensation for the claimant for the lapse of time between the accident or injury and the award of compensation by the court (or time of settlement). Special damages and general damages are treated differently in that they have different periods and rates of interest. Of course, only past losses are considered for interest; future losses will not attract interest.

Special damages

(See 'Compensation for financial loss and expenses up to the date of trial or settlement', above)

> Period: from the date of the accident to trial (or date of settlement)

> Rate: half the High Court Special Investment Account rate (currently 7 per cent)

General damages

(See 'Compensation for 'pain, suffering and loss of amenity'', above)

> Period: from the date of issue of the claim

Highlight

The court has the power to award interest on damages claims.

Rate: currently 3 per cent.

Insurance payouts and other deductions

Insurance payouts are ignored by the court: a defendant cannot take advantage of the fact that he has injured and caused loss to a claimant who has received or who will receive a sum of money from his insurers. The court simply looks at the liability between the claimant and defendant. But the claimant who receives damages will, in due course, under his contract of insurance, have to repay his insurer for any payouts made.

Similarly, pension payments and charitable donations, gifts or grants that are received by the claimant are ignored in the calculation of damages awards. However, where an employer is liable for an employee's injury, any redundancy payment (or part of that redundancy payment) may be deducted.

Provisional damages awards

The courts have power in certain cases to consider and award damages in two tranches. This will be where there is a 'measurable' chance that the claimant will in the future, as a result of the accident or injury, develop a serious disease or that his condition will seriously deteriorate. Such a future development must be over and above the normal development of the disease, so as to justify the court looking twice at the issue of damages. In practical terms the first (or 'provisional') award will therefore not be a 'once and for all' award. This power allows the court to be more accurate in difficult cases where the injuries have an uncertain outcome.

Interim payments

A claimant may apply to the court for an order that the defendant pay him a proportion of the likely final award before the trial has taken place. The application is made by Application Notice (see 'Applications in the period before trial', page 109), and copies must be served on the defendant at least 14 days before the hearing date of the application. Both the claimant and defendant may rely on witness statements at the hearing and the judge will consider the evidence contained in statements of case, the Application Notice and witness statements, together with any documentation relied upon.

The claimant must satisfy the following conditions:

- the period for filing the Acknowledgement of Service has expired; *and*

- the defendant is insured for the claim, or the defendant's liability is to be met by an insurer or the Motor Insurers' Bureau, or the defendant is a public body; *or*

- the defendant has admitted liability to pay damages to him, or the court has made a judgment against the defendant with damages to be assessed; *or*

- the court is satisfied that if the claim went to trial, the claimant would obtain judgment for a substantial amount of damages against the defendant.

The court will consider any claim by the defendant that the claimant was 'contributorily negligent' (see 'Contributory negligence', page 51) and also any counterclaim brought.

Criminal injuries

6

The Criminal Injuries Compensation Scheme

Highlight

The current Criminal Injuries Compensation Schem makes payments to the victims of crime from a central fund, to compensate them for injury.

The current Criminal Injuries Compensation Scheme was set up by the government under the Criminal Injuries Compensation Act 1995. As the name suggests, it is a scheme that makes payments to the victims of crime from a central fund, to compensate them for injury. It is a system that is an alternative to the civil claim for damages which is covered by the rest of this guide. Furthermore, it is a scheme that is designed for the layman; it is considered inappropriate for applicants to require lawyers and although, of course, applicants may hire lawyers for advice or representation, no legal costs will be paid by the scheme.

This section gives a brief overview of the scheme. More detailed guidance is set out in the Criminal Injuries Compensation Authority publication *A Guide to the Criminal Injuries Compensation Scheme*. Further guidance is given in the leaflet *Child Abuse and the Criminal Injuries Compensation Scheme*.

Under the rules, any money paid out under the scheme must be repaid to the extent that the applicant later recovers money from the criminal or other government scheme in relation to the injury.

Who qualifies?

Victims of crime and other persons seeking compensation in their own right

Persons who suffered a 'criminal injury' on or after the 1st August 1964, who have not already made an earlier application under the 1990 or other previous schemes, may apply for compensation. The exception to this general rule is that someone who was living with their assailant as a member of the same family may not be awarded compensation, unless the injury in question was sustained on or after the 1st October 1979.

A criminal injury is described as either a crime of violence (including physical attacks, some threats, sexual offences, arson, poisoning), trespass on a railway, or one received as a consequence of apprehending a suspected offender, the prevention of an offence, or assisting a constable who is doing any of those things. Each case will be taken on its own merits.

An 'injury' includes all physical injury and fatal injury. Mental injuries (medically recognised illnesses or conditions) may be compensated, but only if one of the following features also is present:

- the applicant victim's mental injury arises from a physical one;

- the crime put the applicant victim in reasonable fear of immediate physical harm to himself;

- the applicant had a close relationship of love and affection with the victim who suffered criminal injury and witnessed or was present when the victim was injured, or was closely involved in the aftermath (the applicant need not be the direct victim of the crime);

- the crime involved was a sexual offence to which the applicant victim did not in fact consent;

- the applicant was employed on the railways and witnessed and was present when another person was the injured as a result of a criminal trespass on the railway (or was closely involved in its aftermath).

Claims by dependants and relatives of a dead victim of crime

Where the victim of a criminal injury dies, either as a result of the injuries or from another cause, the following people may apply for compensation under the scheme:

- the victim's husband or wife;

- the victim's long-term unmarried partner (of the opposite sex);

- parent;

- child, even if over 18;

- former husband or wife who was financially supported by the victim.

There is provision for compensation to be paid to more than one eligible applicant. Awards where the victim died as a result of the criminal injury will be made up of a 'fatal injury award', a 'dependency award' and an award for loss of parental services as appropriate. A 'fatal injury award' is a set amount: £10,000 where there is only one qualifying applicant, and £5,000 each where there is more than one (not including former dependent spouses). A 'dependency award' is designed to compensate the applicant who was financially dependent on the deceased. The claims officer looks at the earnings, etc., of the victim before his death and calculates the amount of loss suffered by the descendant applicant. Where the victim died from separate causes compensation is based upon the victim's loss of earnings and expenses suffered as a result of the criminal injury not from the death

Claims by parents or guardians on behalf of injured children

Under the law, a child is someone who has not yet had their 18th birthday. A person who has parental responsibility for the child (including the local authority, where appropriate) may apply on behalf of him for compensation. In the rare event of there being no such adult to act, the Official Solicitor may assist. Note that a copy of the child's birth certificate must be enclosed with the application form.

There are similar provisions for a suitable adult to represent a person who is unable, through a mental disorder, to manage his own affairs.

How to make an application

An application is made using a form supplied by the Criminal Injuries Compensation Authority. There are two forms available: Personal Injury and Fatal Injury which can be obtained from:

> The Criminal Injuries Compensation Authority
> Tay House
> 300 Bath Street
> Glasgow
> G2 4JR
>
> Tel 0141 331 2726
> Fax 0141 331 2287

The application should be received by the Authority no longer than two years from the date of the injury. In certain circumstances, the time limit may be waived if the Authority is satisfied that (a) there has been a good reason for the delay and (b) that it is in the interests of justice to do so.

The decision

The assessment process is conducted by Claims Officers. Applicants are expected to co-operate with the Officer who undertakes an investigation. Enquiries may be made of the medical authorities, the police, employers and other relevant bodies, and the application form requires the applicant to give the relevant body authority to discuss the otherwise confidential information. Further information may also be sought; for example, the applicant may be required to undergo a (further) medical examination.

Some factors that are taken into account upon assessment

General considerations:

a) whether the applicant failed to take all reasonable steps to report the relevant crime to the police;

b) whether the applicant failed to co-operate with the police or other body trying to bring the assailant to justice;

c) whether the applicant has co-operated with the Criminal Injuries Compensation Authority;

d) the conduct of the applicant before, during or after the incident (for example, provocation or bad language, a history of violence with the assailant, etc.);

e) the criminal record of the applicant (except 'spent' convictions) which will attract penalty points leading to a percentage reduction at the appropriate level;

f) any other material before the claims officer which makes it inappropriate to make a full or reduced award;

g) whether an award will indirectly benefit the assailant (particularly where the assailant and victim are living in the same household);

h) the amount the applicant has received from the compensation scheme of another country, or Northern Ireland; civil damages or compensation awarded by a criminal court payable by the assailant;

i) the maximum sum that may be awarded to a claimant is £500,000.

The 'standard amount of compensation':

a) whether or not there is a single injury or multiple injuries to be considered;

b) the nature of the injury.

Loss of earnings:

a) whether or not the applicant has lost earnings or earning capacity for 28 weeks or more as a result of his injury (loss of earnings will not be compensated if the incapacity/inability to work has lasted for less than 28 weeks);

b) the appropriate length of lost earnings or earning capacity payment period (being more than 28 weeks);

c) any salary fees or other payment from work received (or which should have been received) by the applicant;

d)   any changes to the applicant's pension rights;

e)   the amount of social security benefits received;

f)   insurance payments received.

Special expenses:

a)   whether or not the applicant has lost earnings or earning capacity for longer than 28 weeks (special expenses will not be compensated if the incapacity/inability to work has lasted for less than 28 weeks);

b)   loss or damage to equipment belonging to the applicant which he used as a physical aid (such as glasses, wheelchair, etc.);

c)   NHS costs;

d)   private medical costs, where it was reasonable to 'go private' and the amount charged is reasonable;

e)   reasonable costs of special equipment, adaptations of accommodation, costs of care (whether or not at home or in a residential establishment);

f)   the loss of earnings, loss of earning capacity or additional costs of a relative or friend of the applicant who undertakes care of him free of charge, and the level of care provided;

g)   whether such costs are ongoing and if so, what figure is appropriate to cover future expenses.

The amount of the standard award: 'the tariff'

The standard award for the injury is worked out by reference to a table, known as 'the tariff'. Minor multiple injuries attract a 'level 1' award and are defined in 'Note 1' to the tariff. More serious separate multiple injuries are calculated as follows:

the full amount for the injury attracting the highest level of award

+

10% of the amount attracting the next highest level of award

+

5% of the amount attracting the third-highest level of award

= the award

Appendices

Appendix 1: Sample 1 – Driver's claim for damages against another driver

IN THE ANYTOWN COUNTY COURT

B E T W E E N

MRS JOEY SILVER

Claimant

and

MR MARC DE TROP

Defendant

PARTICULARS OF CLAIM

1. The Claimant was at all material times the [*owner*] and driver of a [*make, model colour and registration number of his vehicle*].

2. The Defendant was at all material times the driver of a [*make, model, colour and registration number*].

3. At about [*time*] on the [*date*] the parties were involved in a collision at the [*describe the place of the accident by reference to road names, road numbers or other local references (such as the 'Dog-and-Duck' roundabout)*] in which the Defendant's car collided with the [*rear, side, front etc*] of the Claimant's car.

4. The said collision was caused by the negligence of the Defendant in that he:

PARTICULARS OF NEGLIGENCE[1]

[*a*) *drove too fast in all the circumstances*
b) *failed to keep any or proper lookout*
c) *overtook the Claimant's vehicle when it was unsafe to do so*
d) *crossed into the path of the Claimant's correctly proceeding vehicle*
e) *failed to observe the Claimant's right of way and accord the Claimant precedence*
f) *failed to maintain lane discipline*
g) *failed to stop steer or otherwise control his vehicle so as to avoid colliding with the Claimant's vehicle*

[1] The following is a list of sample allegations. Not all of them will apply to each case. They demonstrate how the claimant must analyse the accident in terms of precise allegations of wrong-doing. The Particulars of Claim must 'tell the story' of the accident and list the facts the court will hear.

(Continued on next page)

Appendix 1: Sample 1 – Driver's claim for damages against another driver (contd)

h) failed to comply with the [red light showing to him/stop sign/solid white line]

i) reversed into the claimant's car

j) failed to indicate his intention/the presence of his vehicle adequately or at all

k) failed to heed the warning/indication given by the Claimant's vehicle

l) drove a vehicle with defective breaks knowing that the said breaks were defective

m) failed to cause the vehicles breaks to be adequately maintained.]

5. The Claimant intends to place evidence before the court pursuant to Section 11 of the Civil Evidence Act 1968 that the Defendant was on [date] at [name and address of the convicting court] convicted of [name of the offence]. The said conviction is relevant to the issue of the Defendant's liability for negligent driving as alleged above.[2]

6. By reason of the above matters the Claimant suffered injury loss and damage:

PARTICULARS OF INJURY

[here give a brief description of the injuries suffered; listing the initial injury, past and anticipated future treatment, level of care and assistance provided already and expected in the future, loss of amenity (see Section 5.1), the level of disruption to working life and the prognosis]

The medical report of [name] is attached hereto.

PARTICULARS OF LOSS

See the Schedule of Special and General Damage attached hereto.

7. And the Claimant claims interest upon such damages as the court shall award at a rate and for such a period as the court thinks fit, pursuant to [Section 69 of the County Courts Act 1984] [Section 35A of the Supreme Court Act].[3]

(Continued on next page)

Appendix 1: Sample 1 – Driver's claim for damages against another driver (contd)

AND the Claimant claims

a) Damages [*less than £5,000/more than £5,000 but less than £15,000/more than £15,000*]

b) Interest as set out above.

STATEMENT OF TRUTH

I believe that the facts stated in these particulars of claim are true.

Full name _____

Name and address of Solicitors' firm [*if used*] _____

_____

_____

Signed _____

ADDRESS FOR SERVICE OF DOCUMENTS

[*Address*]

Appendix 1: Sample 2 – Pedestrian's claim against a driver

[1] The following is a list of sample allegations. Not all of them will apply to each case. You may have to add appropriate allegations to describe how the defendant has been negligent. The claimant must analyse the accident and set out the precise allegations of wrongdoing. The Particulars must 'tell the story' of the accident and list all the facts the court will hear in evidence.

IN THE ANYTOWN COUNTY COURT
B E T W E E N

MRS JOEY SILVER

Claimant

and

MR MARC DE TROP

Defendant

PARTICULARS OF CLAIM

---

1. The Defendant was the driver of a [*make, model, colour and registration number of his vehicle*] at [*place*] on [*date*] at about [*time*]. The Claimant was walking [*describe where*] when the Defendant drove his vehicle into collision with her, knocking her down.

PARTICULARS OF NEGLIGENCE

[a) *drove too fast in all the circumstances*

b) *failed to keep any or proper lookout for pedestrians such as the Claimant*

c) *overtook another vehicle within the zigzag lines of a pedestrian crossing*

d) *failed to accord the Claimant precedence on the zebra crossing*

e) *failed to comply with the red light showing to him at the pelican/toucan/puffin crossing*

f) *failed to accord the Claimant precedence on the pelican crossing [whilst the amber light was flashing] [when the amber light had finished flashing and a green light was showing whilst the Claimant was still crossing]*

g) *failed to stop steer or otherwise control his vehicle so as to avoid colliding with the Claimant*

h) *reversed into the Claimant*

i) *failed to indicate his intention/the presence of his vehicle adequately or at all*

j) *drove a vehicle with defective breaks knowing that the said breaks were defective*

k) *failed to cause his vehicle's breaks to be adequately maintained.*[1]

(Continued on next page)

2. The Claimant intends to place evidence before the court pursuant to Section 11 of the Civil Evidence Act 1968 that the Defendant was on [*date*] at [*name and address of the convicting court*] convicted of [*name of the offence*]. The said conviction is relevant to the issue of the Defendant's liability for negligent driving as alleged above.[2]

3. By reason of the above matters the Claimant suffered injury loss and damage:

PARTICULARS OF INJURY

[*here give a brief description of the injuries suffered; listing the initial injury, past and anticipated future treatment, level of care and assistance provided already and expected in the future, loss of amenity (see Section 5.1), the level of disruption to working life and the prognosis*]

The medical report of [*name*] is attached hereto.

PARTICULARS OF LOSS

See the Schedule of Special and General Damage attached to this Particulars of Claim.

4. And the Claimant claims interest upon such damages as the court shall award at a rate and for such a period as the court thinks fit, pursuant to [Section 69 of the County Courts Act 1984] [Section 35A of the Supreme Court Act 1981].[3]

AND the Claimant claims

a) Damages [*less than £5,000/more than £5,000 but less than £15,000/more than £15,000*]
b) Interest as set out above.

[2] Omit this paragraph if it is inapplicable to your case.

[3] If the case is brought in the High Court the reference is to s.35A of the Supreme Court Act 1981; in the County Court the power to award interest is created by s.69 of the County Courts Act; delete as applicable.

(Continued on next page)

STATEMENT OF TRUTH
I believe that the facts stated in these particulars of claim are true.

Full name _____

Name and address of Solicitors' firm [*if used*] _____

_____

_____

Signed _____

ADDRESS FOR SERVICE OF DOCUMENTS
[*Address*]

Appendix 1: Sample 3 – Bus passenger's claim against bus company alleging negligence and breach of statutory duty

IN THE ANYTOWN COUNTY COURT

B E T W E E N

MRS JOEY SILVER

Claimant

and

THE ANYTOWN BUS COMPANY LIMITED

Defendant

PARTICULARS OF CLAIM

---

1. The Defendant was at all relevant times the owner of a [*describe the bus by type or registration number*] ('the bus'[1]) which was travelling on Route [*number*] in [*town*] on [*date*] as a public service vehicle.

2. The Public Service Vehicles (Conduct of Drivers, Inspectors, Conductors and Passengers) Regulations 1990 ('the Regulations') applied to the bus driver [*and conductor*] who were the Defendant's employees or agents.

3. On the [*date*] the Claimant, a paying passenger, [*lawfully boarded/attempted to board*] the bus when it stopped at a bus stop situated at [*road or place*].

4. [*Describe what happened; what you did, what the driver and conductor did, the actions of any fellow passengers (if relevant) and what happened to the bus*]

5. The Claimant relies upon the fact of the accident as evidence of negligence on the part of the Defendants, their employee(s) or agents. Alternatively, the Defendants, their employee(s) or agents were in breach of statutory duty and/or negligent in that:

PARTICULARS OF NEGLIGENCE[2]

[a) the Defendant failed to instruct their driver [*and/or conductor*], adequately or at all, as to the proper procedure to be adopted at bus stops
b) the driver drove away from the bus stop before receiving any bell or other signal from the conductor

[1] It is better to use a short description throughout, rather than repeated long-winded definitions. The short description should be identified and defined carefully at the outset. This example is perhaps over-careful, as in this set of circumstances there is only one bus. In some situations the facts might be much more complicated and in order to tell the story with clarity careful use of defining terminology is particularly important. In complex cases therefore you would expect to see terms such as 'the first incident', the 'second bus', the 'third payment', etc.

[2] These are samples, some (or even all) may not be relevant to your case; it is important to analyse the facts carefully and decide exactly who has failed in their duty of care, and how.

(Continued on next page)

Appendix 1: Sample 3 – Bus passenger's claim against bus company alleging negligence and breach of statutory duty (contd)

[3] This example only cites one regulation; in your case the bus company might have breached a different statutory duty. To identify the correct regulation(s) from the outset always look at the Regulations before you draft your Particulars of Claim.

c) the driver failed to check whether the Claimant had moved fully onto the bus before he operated the switch to close the door

d) the driver drove away from the bus stop without due regard for people who were on or in the act of boarding the bus

e) the driver failed to give any or adequate warning that he was about to drive the bus away from the stop

f) the driver failed to pay any or sufficient regard to the fact that the bus had an open back

g) the conductor failed to give any or proper warning that the bus was about to move

h) the conductor failed to pay any or sufficient regard to the fact that the bus had an open back

i) the conductor failed to warn the driver, adequately or at all, that not everyone on or in the act of boarding the bus was in a safe position

j) the conductor failed to ensure that all the passengers had boarded the bus safely

k) the conductor failed to monitor and control, adequately or at all, the number of passengers standing in the rear doorway.]

PARTICULARS OF BREACH OF STATUTORY DUTY[3]

[l) the Defendant's driver failed to take all reasonable precautions to ensure the safety of passengers on or entering the bus, including the Claimant, contrary to regulation 5(1) of the Regulations

m) the Defendant's conductor failed to take all reasonable precautions to ensure the safety of passengers on or entering the bus, including the Claimant contrary to regulation 5(1) of the Regulations.]

6. By reason of all the matters complained of above, the Claimant has suffered pain and injury and sustained loss and damage;

PARTICULARS OF INJURY

[here give a brief description of the injuries suffered; listing the initial injury, past and anticipated future treatment, level of care and assistance provided already and expected in the future, loss of amenity (see Section 5.1), the level of disruption to working life and the prognosis]

(Continued on next page)

The medical report of [*name*] is attached hereto.

PARTICULARS OF LOSS

See the Schedule of Special and General Damage attached to this Particulars of Claim.

7. The Claimant is entitled to and claims interest on the amount found to be due to her pursuant to [*section 69 of the County Courts Act 1984/section 35A of the Supreme Court Act 1981*].[4]

AND the Claimant claims

a) Damages [*less than £5,000/more than £5,000 but less than £15,000/more than £15,000*]
b) Interest as set out above.

STATEMENT OF TRUTH
I believe that the facts stated in these particulars of claim are true.

Full name _____

Name and address of Solicitors' firm [*if used*] _____

_____

_____

Signed _____

ADDRESS FOR SERVICE OF DOCUMENTS
[*Address*]

[4] Interest for County Court Cases may be awarded under the County Courts Act 1984; the High Court power to award interest is given by The Supreme Court Act 1981 – delete as applicable..

Appendix 1: Sample 4 – Pedestrian's claim against the highway authority for a tripping accident

[1] The purpose of the Particulars of Claim is to paint a picture in words; you must identify exactly what you were doing just before the accident and describe very precisely where the accident happened.

IN THE ANYTOWN COUNTY COURT

B E T W E E N

MRS JOEY SILVER

Claimant

and

SMALLSHIRE DISTRICT COUNCIL

Defendant

PARTICULARS OF CLAIM[1]

---

1. The Defendant was at all relevant time the highway authority responsible for the [*carriageway/pavement*] which is part of [*road or street name, town and county*]. That road is a highway within the meaning of the Highways Act 1980.

2. At [*time*] on [*date*] the Claimant was [*walking/driving her car/riding her pushbike/motorbike/horse, etc.*] on the [*northern pavement/left-hand side of the carriageway/right-hand lane in accordance with the one-way system which operates at that point[1]*] travelling [*in the direction of the town-centre/towards the junction of X Street with Y Road/in a westerly direction*].

3. Whilst the Claimant was thus travelling [*she/her car/motorbike/horse*] [*describe what happened. Include a measurement of the hole or other defect, and describe how deep or protruding the hazard was*].

4. The accident was caused by the negligence and/or breach of statutory duty of the Defendant, its employees or agents in that they

---

PARTICULARS OF NEGLIGENCE

---

[a] *allowed a [pothole/trench/uneven surface] in the [road/pavement] to continue in existence*

b) *failed to [fill in the pothole/trench] [repair and make good the uneven surface] adequately [or at all]*

c) *failed to resurface the road*

d) *failed to warn users of the highway such as the Claimant of the existence*

(Continued on next page)

of the [pothole/trench/uneven surface] by way of signs, notices, bollards, lights or other appropriate means

e) allowed the road to become or remain unsafe for road users including the Claimant

f) failed to cause road users including the Claimant to avoid the danger created by the [pothole/trench/uneven surface] by way of signs, barriers, fencing, brightly coloured tape, bollards or otherwise directing them to keep clear of it

g) exposed the Claimant to a danger or hazard and/or risk of injury.]

PARTICULARS OF BREACH OF STATUTORY DUTY

[h) by reason of all the matters set out above, the Defendant has failed to maintain the highway contrary to section 41 of the Highways Act 1980.]

5. As a result of the matters set out above the Claimant, whose date of birth is [date] and was [age] at the time of the accident, suffered injury, loss and damage.

PARTICULARS OF INJURY

[here give a brief description of the injuries suffered; listing the initial injury, past and anticipated future treatment, level of care and assistance provided already and expected in the future, loss of amenity (see Section 5.1), the level of disruption to working life and the prognosis]

The medical report of [name] is attached hereto.

PARTICULARS OF LOSS

See the Schedule of Special and General Damage attached to this Particulars of Claim.

6. The Claimant is entitled to and claims interest upon such damages as the court shall award at such a rate and for such a period as the court thinks fit,

(Continued on next page)

Appendix 1: Sample 4 – Pedestrian's claim against the highway authority for a tripping accident (contd)

pursuant to [Section 69 of the County Courts Act 1984] [Section 35A of the Supreme Court Act 1981][2]

AND the Claimant claims

a) Damages [*less than £5,000/more than £5,000 but less than £15,000/more than £15,000*]

b) Interest as set out above.

STATEMENT OF TRUTH
I believe that the facts stated in these particulars of claim are true.

Full name _____

Name and address of Solicitors' firm [*if used*] _____

_____

_____

Signed _____

ADDRESS FOR SERVICE OF DOCUMENTS
[*Address*]

Appendix 1: Sample 5 – Tenant's claim against landlord for injuries arising from defects in rented property (appearing after tenant moved in)

IN THE ANYTOWN COUNTY COURT

B E T W E E N

MRS JOEY SILVER

Claimant

and

[*name of landlord*]

Defendant

_____

PARTICULARS OF CLAIM
_____

1. On [*date*] the Defendant granted a lease of the dwelling house at [*full address of the property*] to the Claimant. The terms of the lease included [*state how long the lease was to run, who much the rent was and how often it had to be paid*].

2. It was an express term[1] of the lease that the landlord [*here quote the term making the landlord responsible for the relevant repairs*]. Additionally or alternatively a repairing covenant was implied into the lease by section 11 of the Landlord and Tenant Act 1985.[2] Additionally or alternatively, the lease gives the landlord the right to enter the premises in order to carry out maintenance or repair work.[3]

3. On [*say when the defect arose*] [*describe the nature of the defect*]. The Claimant told the landlord of the existence of the defect on [*list each occasion the landlord was notified*] by [*letter/fax/e-mail/telephone, etc.*].

4. In breach of the matter(s) set out in paragraph 2 above the Defendant;

_____

PARTICULARS OF NEGLIGENCE
_____

[*list here all the things the landlord has done to make the defect worse, and/or failed to do to in order to make things better.*]

[1] i.e. openly agreed at the outset orally or listed as one of the agreed terms of the written tenancy agreement.

[2] Section 11 lays the responsibility for keeping the structure and exterior of the property and various installations in repair on the landlord. It is not relevant to the state of any other item or part of the building leased. Section 11 will also apply only if the property is residential (a 'dwelling house') and the length of the lease is less than 7 years.

[3] If this clause is found in the lease (or was promised orally) section 4 of the Defective Premises Act 1972 places upon the landlord the duty to take such steps as are reasonable in the circumstances to make all those (such as the Claimant) who might reasonably be affected by the disrepair reasonably safe.

(Continued on next page)

Appendix 1: Sample 5 – Tenant's claim against landlord for injuries arising from defects in rented property (appearing after tenant moved in) (contd)

[4] If the case is brought in the County Court the reference should be to s.69 County Courts Act 1984; for cases in the High Court the power to award interest is created by s.35A Supreme Court Act 1981; delete as appropriate.

PARTICULARS OF BREACH OF STATUTORY DUTY

[*List here all those factors which suggest the landlord has not taken reasonable care of the safety of people like you.*]

5. As a result of the matters set out above the Claimant, whose date of birth is [*date*], suffered personal injury, loss and damage.

PARTICULARS OF INJURY

[*here give a brief description of the injuries suffered; listing the initial diagnosis, past and anticipated future treatment, level of care and assistance provided already and expected in the future, loss of amenity (see Section 5.1), the level of disruption to working and home life and the prognosis*]

The medical report of [*name*] is attached hereto.

PARTICULARS OF LOSS

Please see the Schedule of Special and General Damage attached to this Particulars of Claim.

6. The Claimant is entitled to and claims interest upon such damages as the court shall award at such a rate and for such a period as the court thinks fit, pursuant to [*Section 69 of the County Courts Act 1984*] [*Section 35A of the Supreme Court Act 1981*].[4]

AND the Claimant claims

a) Damages [*less than £5,000/more than £5,000 but less than £15,000/more than £15,000*]
b) Interest as set out above.

(Continued on next page)

Appendix 1: Sample 5 – Tenant's claim against landlord for injuries arising from defects in rented property (appearing after tenant moved in) (contd)

STATEMENT OF TRUTH
I believe that the facts stated in these particulars of claim are true.

Full name _____

Name and address of Solicitors' firm [*if used*] _____

_____

_____

Signed _____

ADDRESS FOR SERVICE OF DOCUMENTS
[*Address*]

How to use this Appendix

Form N9D should be returned to the court if you intend to defend the claim. If there is room then write in the boxes provided and continue on a separate sheet with the claim number written clearly in the top right-hand corner. Alternatively write the whole of your defence (and counterclaim if appropriate) on separate sheets of paper using the suggested layout below.

The defendant should attach any document he relies upon to the Defence. The following matters must be contained in the Defence itself (you might need to add further matters to make your position clear):

- which facts you agree with;

- which facts you neither admit nor deny but of which you have no knowledge;

- which facts you deny AND your version of what happened;

- a 'Counter-schedule of past and future losses and expenses' setting out which of the items in the claimant's Schedule of past and future losses and expenses you agree with, do 'not admit' or dispute;

- whether you agree with the conclusions of the Claimant's medical expert and if you disagree, why;

- any medical report on the claimant by an expert instructed on your behalf you want to rely on at trial;

- a statement that you intend to rely upon a limitation defence;

- a statement that the claimant was contributorily negligent AND a list of details to support your allegation;

- a statement of truth.

Below is a series of paragraphs which show examples of how to do so. The style is not as important as clarity; it is essential that you let the court know what your case will be, and to do that you must address every item of the claim. The contents of the counterclaim (also known as a Part 20 Claim) are exactly like a claim; therefore for selected examples please refer to Appendix 1.

(Continued on next page)

Appendix 2: Defences (contd)
Layout where the Defence form is not used

IN THE ANYTOWN COUNTY COURT

BETWEEN

Claimant

JOSEPHINE BLOGGS

and

Defendant

JOHN SMITH

DEFENCE

1. [Paragraph]
2. [Paragraph]
3. [Paragraph]
4. [Paragraph]

PARTICULARS OF NEGLIGENCE

5. [Paragraph or sub-paragraphs]
6. [Paragraph]

COUNTERCLAIM

7. [Paragraph]
8. [Paragraph]
9. [Paragraph]

STATEMENT OF TRUTH
I believe that the facts stated in this Defence (and Counterclaim) are true.

Full name _____

Name and address of Solicitors' firm [if used] _____

Signed _____

ADDRESS FOR SERVICE OF DOCUMENTS
[Address]

(Continued on next page)

Sample paragraphs

DEFENCE

1. Asserting that the claimant has not established a cause of action

Without prejudice to the following paragraphs the defendant asserts that the facts set out in the Particulars of Claim do not amount to [*state the relevant 'cause of action'*[1]] and [furthermore, the defendant will argue that [*state the relevant section number and title of Act of Parliament or regulation*] does not apply in the circumstances. [The defendant intends to make an application for Summary Judgment/to strike out the Particulars of Claim].[2]

2. Agreeing particular facts

The defendant admits the following [*here list all the paragraphs you fully agree with, or simply recite all the relevant facts in a list*]:

3. 'Not admitting' a particular fact

The defendant does not have any knowledge of the following facts and therefore is unable to admit or deny them [*here set out all the facts alleged in a list*].

4. Denying certain facts and putting forward alternative facts

The defendant denies that [*set out the allegation*]. The [defendant/ name of other witness*] will give evidence to show that [*set out your version of what happened*].

[*repeat for each allegation in dispute*]

5. Denying liability

In all the circumstances the defendant denies that he [*was negligent/in breach of a statutory duty/in breach of contract/assaulted the claimant/ harassed the claimant*] as alleged in the Particulars of Claim or at all.

6. Asserting a statutory defence

The defendant at all times acted reasonably/took reasonable steps to ensure [   ] in that he did: [*set out here*].

[1] For a definition of 'cause of action' see the Glossary.

[2] See page 95, 'Cutting litigation short'; when can a trial be avoided?'

(Continued on next page)

7. The Counter-schedule of past losses and expenses

The defendant attaches to this document a Counter-Schedule of Past and future expenses and losses.[3]

8. Disputing the medical report

The defendant disputes the medical report of [*name*] attached to the Particulars of Claim in the following ways.

[*list*]

9. Relying on your own expert evidence

The defendant disputes the medical report of [*name*] attached to the Particulars of Claim and seeks to rely on the report of [*name and qualifications*] which is attached to this Defence.

10. Relying on expiry of the relevant limitation period

The claimant's claim is barred by the [*section number* Limitation Act 1980/*other appropriate legislation*].

11. Asserting that the claimant has been contributorily negligent

Further, and alternatively to the matters set out above, in the circumstances the claimant was wholly or partly responsible for the accident.

PARTICULARS OF NEGLIGENCE

[*set out here a list of the ways in which the claimant failed to take reasonable care of his own safety; See the examples of Particulars of Negligence in Appendix 1*]

12. Counterclaiming (Part 20 claim)

The defendant relies on the matters set out below by way of set off and counterclaim.

COUNTERCLAIM

[*A counterclaim is set out in the same way as the Particulars of Claim, because in respect of the counterclaim the defendant has become the 'claimant' and the claimant is the 'defendant' to it. For examples of Particulars of Claim see Appendix 1*]

Appendix 3: Personal injury protocol: examples of types of relevant documents – fast track disclosure

Road Traffic Act Cases

Section A

In all cases where liability is at issue –

(i)   Documents identifying nature, extent and location of damage to defendant's vehicle where there is any dispute about point of impact.

(ii)   MOT certificate where relevant.

(iii)   Maintenance records where vehicle defect is alleged or it is alleged by defendant that there was an unforeseen defect which caused or contributed to the accident.

Section B

Accident involving commercial vehicle as potential defendant –

(i)   Tachograph charts or entry from individual control book.

(ii)   Maintenance and repair records required for operators' licence where vehicle defect is alleged or it is alleged by defendants that there was an unforeseen defect which caused or contributed to the accident.

Section C

Cases against local authorities where highway design defect is alleged.

Documents produced to comply with Section 39 of the Road Traffic Act 1938 in respect of the duty designed to promote road safety to include studies into road accidents in the relevant area and documents relating to measures recommended to prevent accidents in the relevant area.

Highway tripping claims

Documents from Highway Authority for a period of 12 months prior to the accident –

(i)   Records of inspection for the relevant stretch of highway.

(ii)   Maintenance records including records of independent contractors working in relevant area.

(iii)   Records of the minutes of Highway Authority meetings where maintenance or repair policy has been discussed or decided.

(Continued on next page)

(iv)   Records of complaints about the state of highways.

(v)   Records of other accidents that have occurred on the relevant stretch of highway.

Workplace claims

(i)   Accident book entry.

(ii)   First aider report.

(iii)   Surgery record.

(iv)   Foreman/supervisor accident report

(v)   Safety representatives accident report.

(vi)   RIDDOR report to HSE.

(vii)   Other communications between defendants and HSE.

(viii)   Minutes of Health and Safety Committee meeting(s) where accident/matter considered.

(ix)   Report to DSS.

(x)   Documents listed above relative to any previous accident/matter identified by the claimant and relied upon as proof of negligence.

(xi)   Earnings information where defendant is employer.

Documents produced to comply with requirements of the Management of Health and Safety at Work Regulations 1992 –

(i)   Pre-accident Risk Assessment required by Regulation 3.

(ii)   Post-accident Re-Assessment required by Regulation 3.

(iii)   Accident Investigation Report prepared in implementing the requirements of Regulations 4, 6 and 9.

(iv)   Health Surveillance Records in appropriate cases required by Regulation 5.

(v)   Information provided to employees under Regulation 8.

(vi)   Documents relating to the employees' health and safety training required by Regulation 11.

(Continued on next page)

Workplace claims – disclosure where specific regulations apply

Section A – Workplace (Health, Safety and Welfare)
Regulations 1992

(i)   Repair and maintenance records required by Regulation 5.

(ii)   Housekeeping records to comply with the requirements of Regulation 9.

(iii) Hazard warning signs or notices to comply with Regulation 17 (Traffic Routes)

Section B – Provision and Use
of Work Equipment Regulations 1992

(i)   Manufacturers' specifications and instructions in respect of relevant work equipment establishing its suitability to comply with Regulation 5.

(ii)   Maintenance log/maintenance records required to comply with Regulation 6.

(iii) Documents providing information and instructions to employees to comply with Regulation 8.

(iv)   Documents provided to the employee in respect of training for use to comply with Regulation 9.

(v)   Any notice, sign or document relied upon as a defence to alleged breaches of Regulations 14 to 18 dealing with controls and control systems.

(vi)   Instruction/training documents issued to comply with the requirements of Regulation 22 insofar as it deals with maintenance operations where the machinery is not shut down.

(vii) Copies of markings required to comply with Regulation 23.

(viii) Copies of warnings required to comply with Regulation 24.

Section C – Personal Protective Equipment
at Work Regulations 1992

(i)   Documents relating to the assessment of the Personal Protective Equipment to comply with Regulation 6.

(Continued on next page)

(ii)   Documents relating to the maintenance and replacement of Personal Protective Equipment to comply with Regulation 7.

(iii) Record of maintenance procedures for Personal Protective Equipment to comply with Regulation 7.

(iv)   Records of tests and examinations of Personal Protective Equipment to comply with Regulation 7.

(v)   Documents providing information, instruction and training in relation to the Personal Protective Equipment to comply with Regulation 9.

(vi)   Instructions for use of Personal Protective Equipment to include the manufacturers' instructions to comply with Regulation 10.

Section D – Manual Handling Operations Regulations 1992

(i)   Manual Handling Risk Assessment carried out to comply with the requirements of Regulation 4(1)(b)(i).

(ii)   Re-assessment carried out post-accident to comply with requirements of Regulation 4(1)(b)(i).

(iii) Documents showing the information provided to the employee to give general indications related to the load and precise indications on the weight of the load and the heaviest side of the load if the centre of gravity was not positioned centrally to comply with Regulation 4(1)(b)(iii).

(iv)   Documents relating to training in respect of manual handling operations and training records.

Section E – Health and Safety (Display Screen Equipment) Regulations 1992

(i)   Analysis of work stations to assess and reduce risks carried out to comply with the requirements of Regulation 2.

(ii)   Re-assessment of analysis of work stations to assess and reduce risks following development of symptoms by the claimant.

(iii) Documents detailing the provision of training including training records to comply with the requirements of Regulation 6.

(Continued on next page)

(iv) Documents providing information to employees to comply with the requirements of Regulation 7.

Section F – Control of Substances
Hazardous to Health Regulations 1988

(i) Risk assessment carried out to comply with the requirements of Regulation 6.

(ii) Reviewed risk assessment carried out to comply with the requirements of Regulation 6.

(iii) Copy labels from containers used for storage handling and disposal of carcinogenics to comply with the requirements of Regulation 7(2A)(h).

(iv) Warning signs identifying designation of areas and installations which may be contaminated by carcinogenics to comply with the requirements of Regulation 7(2A)(h)

(v) Documents relating to the assessment of the Personal Protective Equipment to comply with Regulation 7(3A).

(vi) Documents relating to the maintenance and replacement of Personal Protective Equipment to comply with Regulation 7(3A).

(vii) Records of maintenance procedures for Personal Protective Equipment to comply with Regulation 7(3A).

(viii) Records of tests and examinations of Personal Protective Equipment to comply with Regulation 7(3A).

(ix) Documents providing information, instruction and training in relation to the Personal Protective Equipment to comply with Regulation 7(3A)

(x) Instructions for use of Personal Protective Equipment to include the manufacturers' instructions to comply with Regulation 7(3A).

(xi) Air monitoring records for substances assigned a maximum exposure limit or occupational exposure standard to comply with the requirements of Regulation 7.

(Continued on next page)

(xii) Maintenance examination and test of control measures records to comply with Regulation 9.

(xiii) Monitoring records to comply with the requirements of Regulation 10.

(xiv) Health surveillance records to comply with the requirements of Regulation 11.

(xv) Documents detailing information, instruction and training including training records for employees to comply with the requirements of Regulation 12.

(xvi) Labels and Health and Safety data sheets supplied to the employers to comply with the CHIP Regulations.

Section G – Construction (Design and Management) Regulations 1994

(i) Notification of a project form (HSE F10) to comply with the requirements of Regulation 7.

(ii) Health and Safety Plan to comply with requirements of Regulation 15.

(iii) Health and Safety file to comply with the requirements of Regulations 12 and 14.

(iv) Information and training records provided to comply with the requirements of Regulation 17.

(v) Records of advice from and views of persons at work to comply with the requirements of Regulation 18.

Section H – Pressure Systems and Transportable Gas Containers Regulations 1989

(i) Information and specimen markings provided to comply with the requirements of Regulation 5.

(ii) Written statements specifying the safe operating limits of a system to comply with the requirements of Regulation 7.

(iii) Copy of the written scheme of examination required to comply with the requirements of Regulation 8.

(Continued on next page)

(iv)   Examination records required to comply with the requirements of Regulation 9.

(v)   Instructions provided for the use of operator to comply with Regulation 11.

(vi)   Records kept to comply with the requirements of Regulation 13.

(vii)   Records kept to comply with the requirements of Regulation 22.

Section I – Lifting Plant and Equipment (Records of Test and Examination, etc.) Regulations 1992

(i)   Record kept to comply with the requirements of Regulation 6.

Section J – The Noise at Work Regulations 1989

(i)   Any risk assessment records required to comply with the requirements of Regulations 4 and 5.

(ii)   Manufacturers' literature in respect of all ear protection made available to claimant to comply with the requirements of Regulation 8.

(iii)   All documents provided to the employee for the provision of information to comply with Regulation 11.

Section K – Construction (Head Protection) Regulations 1989

(i)   Pre-accident assessment of head protection required to comply with Regulation 3(4)

(ii)   Post-accident re-assessment required to comply with Regulation 3(5).

Section L – The Construction (General Provisions) Regulations 1961

(i)   Report prepared following inspections and examinations of excavations, etc. to comply with the requirements of Regulation 9.

(ii)   Report prepared following inspections and examinations of work in cofferdams and caissons to comply with the requirements of Regulations 17 and 18.

Appendix 4: Medical negligence protocol: suggested form for requesting hospital medical records

Civil Litigation Committee

Revised Edition
June 1998

THE LAW
SOCIETY

APPLICATION ON BEHALF OF A PATIENT FOR HOSPITAL MEDICAL RECORDS FOR USE WHEN COURT PROCEEDINGS ARE CONTEMPLATED

PURPOSE OF THE FORMS

This application form and response forms have been prepared by a working party of the Law Society's Civil Litigation Committee and approved by the Department of Health for use in NHS and Trust hospitals.

The purpose of the forms is to standardise and streamline the disclosure of medical records to a patient's solicitors, who are investigating pursuing a personal injury claim against a third party, or a medical negligence claim against the hospital to which the application is addressed and/or other hospitals or general practitioners.

USE OF THE FORMS

Use of the forms is entirely voluntary and does not prejudice any party's right under the Access to Health Records Act 1990, the Data Protection Act 1984, or ss 33 and 34 of the Supreme Court Act 1981. However, it is the Department of Health policy that patients be permitted to see what has been written about them, and that healthcare providers should make arrangements to allow patients to see all their records, not only those covered by the Access to Health Records Act 1990. The aim of the forms is to save time and costs for all concerned for the benefit of the patient and the hospital and in the interests of justice. Use of the forms should make it unnecessary in most cases for there to be exchanges of letters or other enquiries. If there is any unusual matter not covered by the form, the patient's solicitor may write a separate letter at the outset.

CHARGES FOR RECORDS

The Access to Health Records Act 1990 prescribes a maximum fee of £10. Photocopying and postage costs can be charged in addition. No other charges may be made.

The NHS Executive guidance makes it clear to healthcare providers that 'it is a perfectly proper use' of the 1990 Act to request records in that framework for the purpose of potential or actual litigation, whether against a third party or against the hospital or trust.

The 1990 Act does not permit differential rates of charges to be levied if the application is made by the patient, or by a solicitor on his or her behalf, or whether the response to the application is made by the healthcare provider directly (the medical records manager or a claims manager) or by a solicitor.

(Continued on next page)

Appendix 4: Medical negligence protocol: suggested form for requesting hospital medical records *(contd)*

The NHS Executive guidance recommend that the same practice should be followed with regard to charges when the records are provided under a voluntary agreement as under the 1990 Act, except that in those circumstances the £10 access fee will not be appropriate.

THE NHS EXECUTIVE ALSO ADVISES:

That the cost of photocopying may include 'the cost of staff time in making copies' and the costs of running the copier (but not costs of locating and sifting records).

That the common practice of setting a standard rate for an application or charging an administration fee is not acceptable because there will be cases when this fails to comply with the 1990 Act.

RECORDS: WHAT MIGHT BE INCLUDED

X-rays and test results form part of the patient's records. Additional charges for copying X-rays are permissible. If there are large numbers of X-rays, the records officer should check with the patient/solicitor before arranging copying.

Reports on an 'adverse incident' and reports on the patient made for risk management and audit purposes may form part of the records and be discloseable: the exception will be any specific record or report made solely or mainly in connection with an actual or potential claim.

RECORDS: QUALITY STANDARDS
When copying records healthcare providers should ensure:

1. All documents are legible, and complete, if necessary by photocopying at less than 100% size.

2. Documents larger than A4 in the original, e.g. ITU charts, should be reproduced in A3, or reduced to A4 where this retains readability.

3. Documents are only copied on one side of paper, unless the original is two sided.

4. Documents should not be unnecessarily shuffled or bound and holes should not be made in the copied papers.

ENQUIRIES/FURTHER INFORMATION

Any enquiries about the forms should be made initially to the solicitors making the request. Comments on the use and content of the forms should be made to the Secretary, Civil Litigation Committee, The Law Society, 113 Chancery Lane, London WC2A 1PL, telephone 020 7320 5739, or to the NHS Management Executive, Quarry House, Quarry Hill, Leeds LS2 7UE.

The Law Society
May 1998

(Continued on next page)

APPLICATION ON BEHALF OF A PATIENT FOR HOSPITAL MEDICAL RECORDS FOR USE WHEN COURT PROCEEDINGS ARE CONTEMPLATED

This should be completed as fully as possible

Insert Hospital Name and Address

TO: Medical Records Officer

Hospital

1 (a)	Full name of patient (including previous surnames)	
(b)	Address now	
(c)	Address at start of treatment	
(d)	Date of birth (and death, if applicable)	
(e)	Hospital ref. no if available	
(f)	N.I. number, if available	
2	This application is made because the patient is considering	
(a)	a claim against your hospital as detailed in para 7 overleaf	YES/NO
(b)	Pursuing an action against someone else	YES/NO
3	Department(s) where treatment was received	
4	Name(s) of consultant(s) at your hospital in charge of the treatment	
5	Whether treatment at your hospital was private or NHS, wholly or in part	

(Continued on next page)

6	A description of the treatment received, with approximate dates	
7	If the answer to Q2(a) is "Yes" details of	
	(a) the likely nature of the claim,	
	(b) grounds for the claim,	
	(c) approximate dates of the events involved	
8	If the answer to Q2(b) is "Yes" insert	
	(a) the names of the proposed defendants	
	(b) whether legal proceedings yet begun	YES/NO
	(c) if appropriate, details of the claim and action number	
9	We confirm we will pay reasonable copying charges	
10	We request prior details of	
	(a) photocopying and administration charges for medical records	YES/NO
	(b) number of and cost of copying x-ray and scan films	YES/NO

(Continued on next page)

11	Any other relevant information, particular requirements, or any particular documents **not** copies of computerised records)	
	Signature of Solicitor	
	Name	
	Address	
	Ref.	
	Telephone Number	
	Fax Number	

Please print name beneath each signature. Signature by child over 12 but under 18 years also requires signature by parent
Signature of patient
Signature of parent or next friend if appropriate
Signature of personal representative where patient has died

(Continued on next page)

SPECIMEN LETTERS OF CLAIM AND RESPONSE

ANNEX C1 – LETTER OF CLAIM

Essential contents

1. Client's name, address, date of birth, etc.

2. Dates of allegedly negligent treatment

3. Events giving rise to the claim:

   an outline of what happened, including details of other relevant treatments to the client by other healthcare providers

4. Allegation of negligence and causal link with injuries:

   an outline of the allegations or a more detailed list in a complex case; an outline of the causal link between allegations; and the injuries complained of

5. The client's injuries, condition and future prognosis

6. Request for clinical records (if not previously provided)

   use the Law Society form if appropriate or adapt specify the records required if other records are held by other providers, and may be relevant, say so

   State what investigations have been carried out to date, e.g. information from client and witnesses, any complaint and the outcome, if any clinical records have been seen or expert advice obtained

7. The likely value of the claim

   an outline of the main heads of damage, or in straightforward cases the details of loss

Optional information

What investigations have been carried out
An offer to settle without supporting evidence
Suggestions for obtaining expert evidence
Suggestions for meetings, negotiations, discussion or mediation

Possible enclosures

Chronology
Clinical records request form and client's authorisation
Expert report(s)
Schedules of loss and supporting evidence

(Continued on next page)

SPECIMEN LETTERS OF CLAIM AND RESPONSE

ANNEX C2 – LETTER OF RESPONSE

Essential contents

1. **Provide requested records and invoice for copying:**

    explain if records are incomplete or extensive records are held and ask for further instructions
    request additional records from third parties

2. **Comments on events and/or chronology:**

    if events are disputed or the healthcare provider has further information or documents on which they wish to rely, these should be provided, e.g. internal protocol
    details of any further information needed from the patient or a third party should be provided.

3. **If breach of duty and causation are accepted:**

    suggestions might be made for resolving the claim and/or requests for further information
    a response should be made to any offer to settle

4. **If breach of duty and/or causation are denied:**

    a bare denial will not be sufficient. If the healthcare provider has other explanations for what happened, these should be given at least in outline suggestions might be made for the next steps, e.g. further investigations, obtaining expert evidence, meetings/negotiations or mediation, or an invitation to issue proceedings

Optional matters

an offer to settle if the patient has not made one, or a counter offer to the patient's with supporting evidence

Possible enclosures

Clinical records
Annotated chronology
Expert reports

Appendix 5: Pre-action protocol for personal injury claims
Specimen letter of claim

To
Defendant

Dear Sirs

Re: **Claimant's full name**
      Claimant's full address
      Claimant's Clock or Works Number
      Claimant's Employer (name and address)

We are instructed by the above named to claim damages in connection with an **accident at work/road traffic accident/tripping accident** on day of (**year**) at (**place of accident which must be sufficiently detailed to establish location**)

Please confirm the identity of your insurers. Please note that the insurers will need to see this letter as soon as possible and it may affect your insurance cover and/or the conduct of any subsequent legal proceedings if you do not send this letter to them.

The circumstances of the accident are:-
(*brief outline*)

The reason why we are alleging fault is:
(*simple explanation. e.g. defective machine, broken ground*)

A description of our clients' injuries is as follows:-
(*brief outline*)
(*In cases of road traffic accidents*)

Our client (*state hospital reference number*) received treatment for the injuries at (*name and address of hospital*).

He is employed as (*occupation*) and has had the following time off work (*dates of absence*). His approximate weekly income is (*insert if known*)

If you are our client's employers, please provide us with the usual earnings details which will enable us to calculate his financial loss.

We are obtaining a police report and will let you have a copy of the same upon your undertaking to meet half the fee.

We have also sent a letter of claim to (*name and address*) and a copy of that letter is attached. We understand their insurers are (*name, address and claims number if known*)

At this stage of our enquiries we would expect the documents contained in parts (*insert appropriate parts of standard disclosure list*) to be relevant to this action.

A copy of this letter is attached for you to send to your insurers. Finally we expect an acknowledgment of this letter within 21 days by yourselves or your insurers.

Yours faithfully

Appendix 6: Benefits recoverable from the defendant by the Department of Social Security

Under the Social Security (Recovery of Benefits) Act 1997

Benefits relating to earnings:

Disability working allowance
Disablement pension payable under section 103 Social Security
      Administration Act 1992
Incapacity Benefit
Income support
Invalidity pension allowance
Jobseeker's allowance
Reduced earnings allowance
Severe disablement allowance
Sickness benefit
Statutory sick pay (prior to 6th April 1994)
Unemployability supplement
Unemployment benefit

Benefits relating to the cost of care:

Attendance allowance
care component of disability allowance
Disablement pension increase payable under section 104 or 105 of
      the Social Security Act 1992

Benefits relating to loss of mobility:

Mobility allowance
Mobility component of disability allowance

Glossary

Acknowledgement of Service – a form used by a defendant to tell the court that he has received the claim form and Particulars of Claim.

acquittal – the formal order of a criminal court where the accused has been found 'not guilty' of the criminal offence for which he has been tried.

admission, Admission – the word has two meanings: a) the acceptance, in court or correspondence, of a fact by one party, which he then cannot later dispute without permission of the court, or b) a form used by the defendant to tell the court that he does not dispute or deny all or part of the claim.

affidavit, affirmation – a document containing the evidence of a witness who has 'sworn' (by a religious oath) or 'affirmed' (by a secular solemn promise) the truth of the contents.

aggravated damages – a sum unusually awarded by the court over and above the usual compensation to compensate the **claimant** for injury to his feelings of dignity and pride.

allocation – an order of the court assigning the case to one of the three trial tracks: Small Claims, Fast and Multi track.

Allocation Questionnaire – a questionnaire filled out by claimants and defendants to tell the court about the case management aspects of their case (including number of witnesses, estimate length of trial, applications that will be made, number of expert witnesses, etc.) so that the court can allocate the case to the appropriate trial track (Small Claim, Fast and Multi).

Application, Notice of Application – where a party has a particular request to the court relating to the documents of the case (disclosure, witness statements, amendment, etc.), management of the case (summary judgment, default judgment, etc.) or to the conduct of the trial (adjournments, witness evidence, etc.) or the grant of various permissions, he makes an 'application'. Applications are governed by Civil Procedure Rules 1998 Part 23. Pre-trial applications should be made on a form called a Notice of Application.

assault – where a person's deliberate action (not mere words) shows an immediate intention to commit a battery on the victim; an assault does not involve any physical contact with the victim (*see* **battery**).

association, *see* **'unincorporated association'**.

barrister – a lawyer who undertakes specialist advocacy and advisory work; the bulk of the work done by independent barristers is the representation of their clients in court. Barristers cannot take instructions direct from the public; they can generally only act on referral by a solicitor.

battery – the deliberate use of unlawful force on the body of another, ranging from mere touching to the use of physical violence.

breach of contract – failure to fulfil or comply with any term of an agreement.

breach of statutory duty – the failure of a person (or company) to comply with a duty imposed on him (or it) by Act of Parliament or Statutory Instrument.

case management conference – (Multi Track cases) a hearing at court in front of a judge at which all parties attend, and at which the court will try to ascertain the matters which remain in dispute, take decisions as to how the case is to be managed, set timetables and give other appropriate directions.

cause of action – the legal basis of the claim for damages or other remedy. Over time the law has developed a series of situations (such as negligence, breach of contract, breach of statutory duty, assault and battery, harassment, etc.) which give rise to a claim for damages; each cause of action has a very specific meaning and it is for the claimant to prove that the facts of his case amount to a claim in law.

child (formally a '**minor**') – someone who has not yet reached their 18th birthday; on his 18th birthday a child becomes, in law, an adult; a child must conduct litigation through a litigation friend.

civil law, civil courts – the branch of the law dealing with people's rights and remedies against each other, the outcome of successful litigation being damages or some other court order putting right the wrong done to the claimant (*see by contrast* **criminal law**).

Civil Procedure Rules 1998 – the set of rules by which the civil courts (both county courts and the High Court) operate. They consist of 53 Parts each dealing with a specific area, various Practice Directions, a Glossary, **Pre-action Protocols** and some of the old County Court Rules and Rules of the Supreme Court which continue to be in force; the rules can be found in publications by the main legal publishers and from The Stationery Office.

claimant – formerly known as 'the plaintiff'; someone who has brought a claim in the courts against the **defendant** for a remedy such as damages.

Claim Form – the form used by the claimant to initiate his claim (Form N1); it identifies the parties, gives a brief description of the claim and an indication of the value of damages expected.

Community Legal Services Funding – CLSF has superseded Legal Aid; it is funding provided by the government for those who do not have the means to pay for legal advice and representation under the Access to Justice Act 1999; it is not available for most personal injury claims.

company, Ltd, plc – a business which by 'incorporating' (a legal process of registration) assumes its own identity, separate from the owners or share-holders; a company can, through its officers, therefore be negligent, breach contracts, breach statutory duties etc. A company may also be vicariously liable for its employees' actions (*see* **vicarious liability**).

Compensation Recovery Unit clawback – the money that the claimant received in certain DSS benefits between the accident and the trial or settlement, which must be paid back to the DSS out of the damages agreed or awarded.

compromise – an out-of-court settlement of a claim (see **settlement**).

conditional fee agreement (CFA), no-win-no-fee – the agreement between a solicitor and his client that the solicitor will only be paid if the client 'wins' the case (whether he is **claimant** or **defendant**).

contract – a legally binding agreement between two or more parties comprising various terms or separate promises, which may be explicit or may be implied (by the common law or statute); under the contract each party must fulfil the promises he has made, and breaches of those promises will only be lawful in certain circumstances. An unlawful breach of promise will entitle the other party to damages.

contribution – a type of **Part 20 claim** brought by the **defendant** (who becomes known as the Part 20 claimant) against a person (the Part 20 defendant); the Part 20 claimant must prove that the Part 20 defendant is liable either jointly or in his own right for the **claimant's** loss and injury under the Civil Liability (Contribution) Act 1978.

contributory negligence – where the **defendant** proves that the **claimant**'s own negligence (failure to take reasonable care of his own safety in the cir-cumstances) has contributed to the damage or injury suffered; if a court finds that the claimant is partly to blame for his own injury it will assess the percentage blame attributable to the defendant, and reduce the damages accordingly.

conviction – the formal finding of a criminal court (magistrates' or the Crown Court) that the defendant is guilty, either when he is found guilty at trial, or pleads guilty voluntarily.

costs – the legal cost of litigation, including the fees of solicitors, barristers, expert witnesses, court fees and other 'disbursements'.

counterclaim – an example of a **Part 20 claim** (after the **Civil Procedure Rule** governing such claims); a counterclaim is a **claim** for damages or other remedy brought by a **defendant** against the **claimant** or the claimant and another person. Where the claim and counterclaim arise out of the same incident or set of facts the court will usually order that both are heard together in one trial.

criminal law, criminal courts – that part of the law which deals with the state's (The Crown) condemnation and punishment of people who commit criminal offences; criminal law is generally dealt with in the criminal courts, (magistrates' courts or the Crown Court).

cross-examination – the series of questions put to a witness by the other party at trial designed to test the evidence of that witness for inconsistencies or inaccuracies etc. Any witness whose oral or written evidence is put before the court may be cross examined by the other side, although the judge has the power to limit cross-examination (**Civil Procedure Rules 1998** Part 32).

damages – monetary compensation awarded by the court to people who have suffered loss or injury; the person found to be negligent or in breach of duty (or his insurer) pays.

default judgment, judgment in default of defence – an order of the court deeming the **claimant** to have 'won' and usually awarding him the damages sought, or fixing a date for the assessment of the amount to be paid; it can only be obtained in circumstances set out in **Civil Proceedings Rules 1998** Part 12. The **defendant** can apply to **set aside** such a default judgment in circumstances set out in **Civil Proceedings Rules 1998** Part 13.

defence, Defence – a defence is a legal excuse or justification to all or part of the claim; a **defendant's** defence is set out in a document called a Defence, which is designed to assist the court and the **claimant** to know exactly what parts of the **claim** are disputed.

defendant – the person against whom the **claimant** has a **claim**; i.e. the claimant must prove that the defendant is legally liable for his loss and injury.

directions – actions required of a party or parties imposed by the court and set out in an order.

directions hearing – a hearing in front of the judge at a preliminary stage during the preparations for trial at which the parties discuss the management of the case, and the court makes an order directing the parties to take certain actions such as exchange witness statements, etc.; usually will be given a strict timetable for compliance with directions.

disposal hearing – a type of hearing or trial at which the court hears evidence relating only to quantify the amount of damages to be paid (the defendant's liability to pay damages having been decided at an earlier hearing, or having been conceded by the defendant himself).

evidence – material (oral testimony, written testimony, artefacts, measurements or documentation) put before the judge which proves a fact alleged by the **claimant** or **defendant**.

exemplary damages – a sum of money that is over and above the compensation awarded to a **claimant** which marks the court's disapproval of the **defendant's** conduct; they are only awarded in certain types of case (including where the government is a defendant and has acted oppressively, or where the defendant has calculated that he will gain a profit from his wrongdoing even if he has to pay damages).

expert evidence – the evidence (usually oral or written testimony, plus measurements or other observations) of a professional who can assist the court with his opinion from the viewpoint of a particular discipline.

false imprisonment – where the **defendant** unlawfully deprives the **claimant** of his liberty.

Fast Track – a trial track to which medium-size **claims** may be allocated (**allocation**).

firm, *see* **partnership**.

group litigation order – an order of the court made under **Civil Procedure Rules 1998** Part 19 which provides for the joint case management of claims which raise similar or common issues of fact or law.

harassment – a course of conduct by the **defendant** which amounts to harassment of the **claimant**.

hearsay, hearsay evidence – testimony that is not eyewitness but rather is the report of someone else's eyewitness; as in 'Ruth told me that Gary was driving the car' – where 'Ruth told me' is the speaker's direct evidence, and '...Gary was driving the car' is the speaker's hearsay evidence.

Highway Code – a publication issued by the Department of Transport, Local Government and the Regions, and published by The Stationery Office; it contains written guidance for use of the roads (for all road users) and material related to criminal offences.

Indemnity – a type of **Part 20 claim** in which the **defendant** (known as a Part 20 claimant) invokes a contractual right to recoup certain sums – an indemnity – from the Part 20 defendant.

issue of claim – the formal beginning of litigation, when the court stamps the **Claim Form** and notes the date (the date of issue).

judgment – the formal process by which the judge communicates his decision to the parties; it may be automatic in some circumstances (see **default judgment**) but generally is delivered orally (or in writing) at the end of the trial. The judge will tell the parties in his judgments of the findings of fact he has made, and of any rulings of law.

Judicial Studies Board Guidelines – a set of guidelines used by the courts and by lawyers to determine the amount of damages for the 'pain, suffering and loss of amenity' part of a **claim.**

Legal Aid – now defunct, *see* **Community Legal Services Funding.**

limitation, limitation period – the period after the accident or onset of loss and injury in which the **claimant** may bring a **claim**; once the period has expired the **defendant** will be able to raise a defence that the claim is 'statute barred' under the Limitation Act 1980.

listing questionnaire – a questionnaire sent to the parties by the court during the preparations for trial stage; the information sought will assist the court in allocating the appropriate court time for the trial, and dealing with any other trial issues such as witnesses' needs, etc.

litigant-in-person – a party in litigation who is conducting his own case and representing himself, rather than hiring a lawyer to do so.

litigation friend – a person who acts as a representative for a **child** (or **patient**), **claimant** or **defendant** in order to conduct the litigation – including instructing lawyers, complying with court orders, etc.

Mckenzie friend – a layperson (non-lawyer) who may, with the permission of the judge, act as an advisor and moral support to a **litigant-in-person** whilst in court; the McKenzie friend may generally not, however, speak on behalf of the litigant-in-person.

minor, *see* **child**.

mitigation of loss – the duty of the **claimant** to take reasonable steps to lessen his loss or injury where he can.

Motor Insurer's Bureau – industry-wide group of motor insurers who has made various agreements with the government to provide insurance in certain situations.

Multi Track – a trial track to which large or complex **claims** may be allocated (**allocation**).

negligence – a breach of the duty imposed by the common law to take care for the safety of a person; in other words, situations where the law holds the **defendant** liable for the costs and injury caused to the **claimant** by his carelessness.

no-win-no-fee, *see* **conditional fee agreements**.

Ogden Tables – actuarial tables used by lawyers to calculate damages representing future financial loss.

order – the formal decision of the court, consisting of pronouncements and requirements; delivered (usually verbally) by the judge and typed up or 'drawn up' by the court who then sends it to the parties.

pain, suffering and loss of amenity – elements which are taken into to consideration when calculating the amount of damages for injury; 'loss of amenity' is the effect that the injury has on one's ability to carry out the everyday activities and enjoyments of life (housework, personal care, mobility, social interaction, confidence, hobbies, aspirations and expectations, etc.).

Part 20 claim – a claim for damages or other remedy made under Part 20 of the **Civil Procedure Rules 1998**; examples include **counterclaims** and claims for a **contribution** and/or **indemnity**.

Part 36 offer – (Fast and Multi Track claims only) an offer made by the **claimant** or other party in litigation to settle a **claim** under the provisions of Part 36 of the **Civil Procedure Rules 1998** (*see* **settlement**).

Particulars of Claim – a formal document submitted to the court usually with the **claim form** in which the **claimant** gives details of the facts on which his claim is based (including financial losses and costs).

partnership – a relationship between two or more people carrying on a business in common with a view to profit, where the business is not 'incorporated' (or mining in certain areas). The partners are collectively known as a firm and is not the same thing in law as a **company**; however, a firm can employ personnel, and the partners will be legally liable for the acts of their employees (**vicarious liability**) and also for the acts of other partners acting in the course of the business.

patient – a person suffering from a mental disorder (as defined in the Mental Health Act 1983) which renders him incapable of managing and administering his own affairs; a patient must conduct litigation through a **litigation friend**.

payment into court – the payment of a sum of money to the court by the **defendant** or a **Part 20** defendant by way of an offer to settle proceedings under Part 36 of **Civil Procedure Rules 1998** (*see* **settlement**).

personal representatives – a general term used to describe the people who formally wind up the estate of a someone who has died (call in the moneys owing, and pay the appropriate sums to the tax man and beneficiaries, etc.); personal representatives either operate under the deceased's will, in which case they are granted 'probate' and are called 'executors', or they operate under the statutory provisions for intestacy in which case they take out 'letters of administration' and are called 'administrators'.

plaintiff, *see* **claimant**.

pre-action protocol – a code of conduct setting out the steps that potential parties to personal injury litigation must observe before litigation starts; the protocol aims to promote early **settlement**.

pro bono – work that is undertaken by a lawyer for no fee.

representative order – an order of the court made under **Civil Procedure Rules** Part 19 (Part II) where one person is deemed to represent others for the purposes of a case – such an order may be suitable where many potential litigants have the same interests as each other.

Response Pack – the pack of documents sent to the defendant by the court with the **Claim Form**.

retail price index, RPI – an official indicator of indication, produced monthly; the RPI is used by lawyers to calculate what general damages awards are worth is today's money.

settlement – an agreement between the parties to litigation which ends the claim, either before the **claim** begins or at any time (including during the trial) before the judge gives his **judgment**.

Small Claims Track – one of the three trial tracks; normally personal injury claims where the damages for **pain, suffering and loss of amenity** are expected to be £1,000 or less and the total value of the claim is £5,000 or less.

solicitor – a lawyer who undertakes a range of legal services.

solicitor-advocate – a solicitor who has rights of audience in the higher courts, and who therefore may represent a party before the judge at trial.

special damage – the quantifiable costs losses and expenses (though not the legal costs) suffered by the claimant between the accident and the trial or those that he knows he will incur in the future.

standard of proof – where there is a dispute about what happened (i.e. a factual rather than a legal dispute about liability), to find a claim proved, the judge must believe that the claimant's version is probably the correct one. Similarly to prove a defence the judge must find the defendant's version is probably correct. These legal tests applied by the judge to the evidence before him at trial are known as the 'standard of proof'. In civil matters the standard of proof is 'on the balance of probabilities' (as opposed to 'beyond reasonable doubt', which is the criminal standard).

statement of case – a general description for a class of documents used by parties in litigation to set down the precise facts of their respective cases; **claim forms**, **particulars of claim** and **defences** are all examples of statements of case.

statement of truth – a phrase which must be included on certain documents put before the court in which the person whose document it is verifies the contents as true. Statements of truth must be included in Particulars of Claim, defences, application notices and witness statements.

statutory duty – a duty imposed on a person (such as an employer) or a body (such as a highway authority) for the benefit of specific persons (such as employees or road users) by an Act of Parliament or statute. In certain cases a breach of such a duty gives rise to a civil claim for damages; in others a criminal penalty arises.

summary judgment – a judgment obtained by a party under **Civil Procedure Rules 1998** Part 24 at a private hearing (rather than a trial), where he can satisfy the court that his opponent has no real prospect of success and that there is no other compelling reason for there to be a trial.

tort – a Norman French word still used to describe a class of common law civil wrongs; from time to time the law extends the list which includes **negligence, assault, battery, false imprisonment**, etc.

trial – the formal hearing at which the court considers the evidence (oral, written, documentary and physical) relating to the **claim** and **defence**, hears the legal argument and gives a judgment.

unincorporated association – a group of people who have collected together for a particular reason (such as a club) but who have not formed a **partnership (firm)**, **company**, friendly society or industrial society. Often the members are bound by a contractual relationship, or have agreed to abide by a set of rules or constitution. Unincorporated associations may own property, enter contracts and employ people; however, they do so through one or more individuals (such as a club chairman) and since the association takes on no 'legal personality' of its own it cannot be sued as such. Thus members can only sue or be sued individually or through a **representative order**.

vicarious liability – a legal rule which makes the someone legally liable for the (civil) wrongs committed by someone else; thus employers are responsible for the **torts** committed by employees in the course of their employment; the rule enables the **claimant** to claim against the employee for his 'primary' liability, and the employer for his 'vicarious' liability.

'without prejudice' – a statement made by one or more party in litigation (or potential party to litigation) verbally or in correspondence to the other side which is a genuine attempt to settle some or part of the claim. Without prejudice statements generally may not be drawn to the attention of the court.

witness statement – a written statement ordered by the court containing the evidence of a witness and verified by a **statement of truth** by the maker of the statement. Usually, a witness statement, after being formally 'adduced' (in other words identified and confirmed by a witness who has just taken an oath or affirmation) is allowed to be read by the court as the witness's 'evidence in chief'. The statement then becomes the basis for **cross-examination**.

Index

The index covers chapters and appendices. Terms categorise personal injuries. An 'i' after a page number indicates an illustration (or illustration and text).

Notes

More books and software from Law Pack...

Law Pack Form Books are invaluable storehouses of literally hundreds of ready-made legal and business documents, for use at work or at home.

Law Pack Guides are user-friendly, do-it-yourself manuals that take the reader step by step through a specific subject and its procedures. Information, instructions and advice are backed up with example paperwork for guidance.

Home & Family Solicitor

The essential do-it-yourself legal resource for every home. From taking action against a noisy neighbour to drawing up a live-in nanny's employment contract, this Form Book will provide you with the ideal, ready-to-use legal letter or agreement. Covers: Credit & Finance, Employment, Goods, Services & Utilities, Insurance, Personal & Family, Lettings & Property, Local Environment.

301 Legal Forms, Letters & Agreements

Our **best-selling Form Book now in its fifth edition**. It is packed with forms, letters and agreements for legal protection in virtually every situation. It provides a complete do-it-yourself library of 301 ready-to-use legal documents, for business or personal use. Areas covered include Loans & Borrowing, Buying & Selling, Employment, Transfers & Assignments and Tenancy.

User testimonials on 301 Legal Forms, Letters & Agreements:

'A long awaited and needed publication which is a handy reference guide for almost every occurrence'
Ms R G Jones, Bank Officer,
Gillingham, Kent.

'Absolutely brilliant. Would be lost without it. Ideal for any business'
Richard Shaw, Company Director, Leeds.

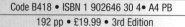

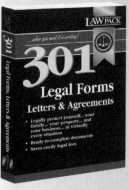

Code B418 • ISBN 1 902646 30 4 • A4 PB
192 pp • £19.99 • 3rd Edition

Code B402 • ISBN 1 902646 72 X • A4 PB
358 pp • £19.99 • 7th Edition

... to order, simply call 020 7940 7000 or visit www.lawpack.co.uk

Limited Company

Do you want to set up a business? This Guide explains how to set up your own limited company yourself. It is packed with explanations of procedure, and includes examples of Companies House forms, Memorandum and Articles of Association, resolutions and provides answers to all questions. Valid in England and Wales, and Scotland.

Code B405 • ISBN 1 902646 58 4 • 246 x 189mm PB
96 pp • £9.99 • 3rd Edition

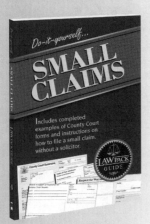

Small Claims

If you want to take action to recover a debt, resolve a contract dispute or make a personal injury claim, you can file your own small claim without a solicitor. This Guide includes clear instructions and advice on how to handle your own case and enforce judgment.

Code B406 • ISBN 1 902646 04 5 • A4 PB
96 pp • £9.99 • 2nd Edition

Employment Law

Whether you are an employer or an employee, you have rights in the workplace. This best-selling Guide is a comprehensive reference source on hiring, wages, employment contracts, termination, discrimination and other important issues. It puts at your fingertips all the important legal points employers and employees should know.

Code B408 • ISBN 1 902646 61 4 • 246 x 189mm PB
148 pp • £9.99 • 4th Edition

... to order, simply call 020 7940 7000 or visit www.lawpack.co.uk

Probate

What happens when someone dies, with or without leaving a Will, and their estate needs to be dealt with? Probate is the process whereby the deceased's executors apply for authority to handle the deceased's assets. This Guide provides the information and instructions needed to obtain a grant of probate, or grant of letters of administration, and administer an estate without the expense of a solicitor.

Code B409 • ISBN 1 902646 27 4 • 246 x 189mm PB
96 pp • £9.99 • 2nd Edition

Divorce

File your own undefended divorce and save legal fees! This Guide explains the process from filing your petition to final decree. Even if there are complications such as young children or contested grounds this Guide will save you time and money.

Code B404 • ISBN 1 902646 05 3 • A4 PB
120 pp • £9.99 • 2nd Edition

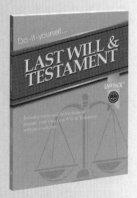

Last Will & Testament

With the help of this Guide writing a Will can be a straightforward matter. It takes the reader step by step through the process of drawing up a Will, while providing background information and advice. Will forms, completed examples and checklists included.

Code B403 • ISBN 1 902646 85 1 • 246 x 189mm PB
88 pp • £9.99 • 3rd Edition

Motoring Law

Whether we like it or not, motoring is fact of everyday life. But how many drivers actually know their rights and those of the police? The Highway Code provides the driving basics. This Law Pack Guide is essential follow-up reading on the motorist's real rights and remedies.

Code B415 • ISBN 1 898217 51 3 • A4 PB
104 pp • £9.99 • 1st Edition

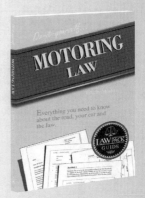

Credit File

Refused credit? Bad credit? We nearly all rely on credit, whether it be with the bank, mortgage lender or credit card company. This Law Pack Guide explains just how credit agencies work, what goes on to your credit file and what legitimate action you can take to improve it. It divulges lenders decision-making processes and blows the lid off 'credit repair' and credit 'blacklists'.

Code B413 • ISBN 1 898217 77 7 • A4 pb
76 pp • £9.99 • 1st Edition

House Buying, Selling and Conveyancing

It isn't true that only those who have gone through long, expensive and involved training can possibly understand the intricacies of house buying, selling and conveyancing. This Law Pack Guide is a new, updated edition of a best-selling book by Joseph Bradshaw, once described in *The Times* as the 'guru of layperson conveyancing', which explains step-by-step just how straightforward the whole process really is. Required reading for all house buyers (or sellers).

Code B412 • ISBN 1 902646 70 3 • 246 x 189mm PB
200 pp • £9.99 • 2nd Edition

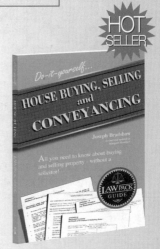

... to order, simply call 020 7940 7000 or visit www.lawpack.co.uk

Law Pack Legal Adviser

Fast answers to nearly all your legal questions! The *Law Pack Legal Adviser* is a comprehensive and succinct guide on the different ways the law influences our everyday lives. It covers such topics as setting up home, children, work, buying goods and services, neighbours, sports, holidays, motoring, money, the police, and the legal system. *Legal Adviser* is a clear and reliable guide to one's rights under the law and is as essential in the home as any standard reference book.

Code B421 • ISBN 1 902646 53 3 • 246 x 189mm PB
300 pp • £15.99 • 1st Edition

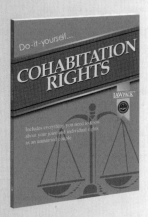

Cohabitation Rights

As more couples choose not to marry, the legal and financial issues they face with children, mortgages, pensions, separation and death become ever more important to understand and address. This book discusses the options in cohabitation agreements and mediation, and provides practical advice for couples.

Code B423 • ISBN 1 902646 52 5 • 246 x 189mm PB
104 pp • £9.99 • 1st Edition

Residential Lettings

Required reading for anyone letting residential property. Covering the legal background and including real-life case studies, this book provides all that a would-be landlord needs to know before letting a flat or house. It covers preparation of the property, finding a tenant, the tenancy agreement, problem tenants, buy-to-let, HMOs and more.

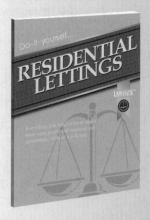

Code B422 • ISBN 1 902646 51 7 • 246 x 189mm PB
120 pp • £9.99 • 1st Edition

... to order, simply call 020 7940 7000 or visit www.lawpack.co.uk

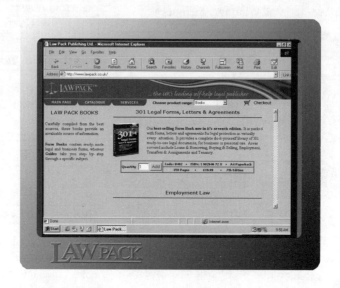